I0568814

Like an Everflowing Stream

Baron Mullis

Like an Everflowing Stream
ISBN: Softcover 978-1-946478-29-0
Copyright © 2017 by Baron Mullis

All rights reserved. No part of this book may be reproduced or transmitted in any form or by any means, electronic or mechanical, including photocopying, recording, or by any information storage and retrieval system, without permission in writing from the publisher.

To order additional copies of this book, contact:

Parson's Porch Books
1-423-475-7308
www.parsonsporch.com

Parson's Porch Books is an imprint of **Parson's Porch & Book Publishers** in Cleveland, Tennessee, which has double focus. We focus on the needs of creative writers who need a professional publisher to get their work to market, **&** we also focus on the needs of others by sharing our profits with those who struggle in poverty to meet their basic needs of food, clothing, shelter and safety.

Like an Everflowing Stream

For Lester

Contents

Part One

Call: Proclamations of Grace

The Church of New Beginnings
John 1:29-42

When I was serving a church in Indianapolis, I had a colleague who was a bit more adventurous than I am and consequently would often take the scenic route for about any drive that he could. Where I would drive straight from Indianapolis to Chicago, Mark would instead wander around through the countryside, taking it all in. (I've never quite understood why he wanted to take in northern Indiana. Southern Indiana is beautiful but northern? It's just flat. There are lots of cornfields. In the winter, it's acres upon acres of corn stubble. With all love and respect to the Hoosiers I know, corn stubble is just not attractive.) Anyhow, in one of his meandering drives he happened on a sight that intrigued and attracted him. He and his wife saw in the distance a pretty ramshackle building that was obviously a church. (Which I suppose is the advantage of living in a flat state – you see things a long way off.) Mark was intrigued so they drove a little closer. As they approached the building, they saw the church had one of those signs out front that can be changed to read different things. This particular church had used their moveable letters to announce the name of the church and Mark said that was what caught his attention. Outside this rundown little building was a marquee that read, "The Church of New Beginnings."

It was the name that intrigued him. He started wondering what a church that really offered new beginnings looked like.

But that's exactly what we claim each week, that we can begin again.

Take for example this couple of fellows who thought they had it all figured out. They had found this preacher, you see. And man, could he preach. He knew just how to combine the right gestures and body language with a compelling message. He could bring just enough heat to the sermon to convince you that it was time to repent. And then, when you repented, he'd take you right out in the river and dunk you on the spot. He had the charisma to know that there is a moment to strike the chord, and he'd nail it every time. He could work up just the right amount of moral indignation to make you jump in alongside him by pointing out the obvious-calling attention to the failings of the government or the church to meet the needs of the people. Let me tell you, he could preach – and not in a high-minded fussy way. So these fellows just warmed right up to him and they became friends. They were standing around, shooting the breeze one day, when out of the blue, their preacher *lost his mind*. At least that's what it seemed like. He said, "Look, here is the Lamb of God." And when he said it, he pointed to this other man, one they'd seen walking around, just like any other guy, and their preacher said, "Here is the lamb of God."

So these two fellows started to follow the other preacher. I guess they stayed back a bit, but it's kind of hard to hide the fact that you're following someone so he turned around to them and said, "What are you looking for?"

Well, you know how it is when someone takes you by surprise. You just say anything…you don't really answer the question that is asked, you try to find a way to save face-you know, like those times when you're staring at someone while trying not to stare at them so that you can figure out how you know them, and then right about the time that you figure out that you've never met them in your life, they notice you've been staring? Well, this preacher turns around to these two fellows who've been following him and says, "What are you looking for?"

So they answered him, "Where are you staying?"

And he says back to them, "Come on and see."

Well, so far, the whole think looks like a comedy of errors, but now it gets really interesting. The two fellows, Andy and John follow this other preacher back to his motel, and they hung out until about four o'clock. Then Andy remembered he was supposed to pick up his brother from work, so he had to get on over to the QuikTrip.

So Andy found his brother Simon, and he said, "You are not going to believe this guy. John says he's the lamb of God. I just spent the afternoon with him, and you've got to meet him. He's the messiah."

So Simon gives Andy the benefit of a doubt and they hop in the pickup truck and head back on over to Cheshire Motor Inn and Simon walks in and Jesus looks up at him and says, "I'm going to call you Rocky." Then the next day Jesus decided he would go to his cousin's wedding in the next county and they went with him.

Does that strike you as just a bit odd? You meet someone and the next day you quit your job and follow him? I may as well own it, that strikes me odd. When I think about the way Andrew and Simon Peter came to follow Jesus and fast-forward it; it strikes me as odd. I can't say for certain that I have the kind of faith that it would take to do that. But that is what happened. Through a series of what must surely have looked like chance encounters, Simon and Andrew end up following Jesus. Only, he's not Simon anymore, Jesus has given him a new name. And in the Bible, the giving of a new name means a new beginning. Something has changed. Now he's Peter, and his whole world has changed.

Peter was changed by his encounter with the lamb of God.

Years ago, another colleague of mine was interviewing with various PNCs around the country and he ended up in conversation with a church up in New Jersey. It too is a rather unremarkable building. So my friend went there to interview and there was one aspect of the sanctuary that he found intriguing. In the pew racks, where we have Bibles and Hymnals, he found both of those things, but in every rack, there was also a box of Kleenex. It struck him as a bit odd, but he didn't say anything about it until later on. When they had finished their interview and just about said everything they had to say, he asked the question. "So why are there boxes of Kleenex in all the pew racks?"

"The Kleenex are there," said the chair of the committee, "because we believe people come here expecting to be moved and changed. A few years ago, we were floundering a bit, we didn't know exactly what our identity was. So we did a study of what was important to the members of the congregation that are here, and what the demographics of the neighborhood suggest is important to our neighbors, and they weren't the same, and so we drew the conclusion that the only way we could revitalize our congregation was to throw our doors wide open and invite the whole neighborhood in. Well, we thought what would happen was that we would assimilate all these folks and make them part of 'our church'. Our nearest neighbor is a rehab clinic, so we knew we'd have recovering addicts if they came to church. We didn't have any LGBT members, but our neighborhood has lots of LGBT living here. We figured we'd just grit our teeth and bear it and eventually we would brainwash them sufficiently that they would think like us. Then the opposite happened. We started to see things through their eyes – through the eyes of an addict, through the eyes of someone pushed out of their own family or pushed to the margin of society. And then we were the ones who were crying in worship."

Peter was changed about his encounter with the lamb of God, but what about us?

The Bible says a lot about change in our hearts. Ours is a faith based on change – personal change and personal growth. We are not static. God expects our faith to engage our living. If we come to church on Sunday morning and leave and go back into our business or our school or our homes and you can't tell any difference between us and the rest of the secular world then I would argue, not much has happened. Maybe we felt good on Sunday, a little holy, and we got our church fix, but if we don't live any differently than the folks who haven't had their names changed, then we might even be wasting our time and God's as well.

Because we too have had our name changed. Just as Simon became Peter, the Rock upon which the church would be built, we too are not as we were. We are now called Christians. When we baptize a child, by the way, that is the question we ask, "What is the Christian name of your child?" We ask because we're calling them by name and saying there's a change. There is a before and an after. The babies can't tell, but the adults we baptize know there's a difference. So we're clear, before we are baptized, or have our children baptized, we are not outside of God's grace – we never are, not for a moment in our lives does God abandon us or ignore us, but in Baptism, we claim for ourselves or our children those promises God has already made. So, if we come to church but we don't integrate Christianity into how we live as people in the world – if we don't reflect the change that has happened to us, then we need to get to work on it and start trying to show God's hand upon us. Because that change is important. We are a place of new beginnings…again and again and again.

I'm quite sure we don't always feel very Christian. I don't sometimes. If you don't feel like a Christian, don't worry about that, C.S. Lewis says. His advice is good sound advice. If you don't feel like a Christian, then just act like one. If you see someone coming and your feelings are not Christian, not charitable and kind, don't worry about that. *Act* as though your feelings are charitable and kind. And keep on acting charitably and kindly, and he said, you will come to the point when it is not an act. There is truth to his words, but we have to do it earnestly and deliberately and constantly. We have to work at acting like Christians – not just here in the church, but elsewhere as well.

It's good advice and it will bear fruit, but that is only half of the good news that our lesson today shares.

There is another side to a new beginning, and that is that God never gives up on any of us. There is nothing that lies outside the scope of God's grace. Do you remember the baptism scene in "O Brother, Where Art Thou?" In it, as Everett, Pete and Delmar are making their way on their Odyssey, Everett and Delmar (in a fit of religious frenzy) get themselves baptized, and when they come up out of the river, Pete and Delmar declare to Everett the preacher told them, "Their sin's done been washed away!" And as naïve and simplistic and simple as it seems, it's the truth!

Our new beginning is truly a new beginning. And that may not sound like great good news to all of us, but I can tell you right now that I know some folks for whom that is good news like the water of life. Because there are sometimes when there is no fixing what has happened, and nothing short of a new beginning is going to change the situation. And the good news of the Gospel is that we can have that new beginning.

Fred Craddock captures it so well, he writes: "When I was pastoring in Tennessee there was a girl about seven years old who came to our church regularly, to Sunday School and sometimes her parents let her stay for the worship service. They didn't come. We had a circular drive at that church. It was built for people who let their children off and drove on. We didn't want to inconvenience them, so we had a circular drive. But they were very faithful, Mom and Dad. They had moved here from New Jersey with the chemical plant. He was upwardly mobile, they were both very ambitious, and they didn't come to church. There wasn't really any need for that, I guess. But on Saturday nights, the whole town knew of their parties. They gave parties, not for entertainment, but as part of the upwardly mobile thing. That determined who was invited – the right people, the one just above, finally on up to the boss. And those parties were full of drinking and wild and vulgar things. Everybody knew. But there was a beautiful girl every Sunday.

One Sunday morning, I looked out and she was there, and I thought, 'well, she's with her friends,' but there were Mom and Dad. And after the sermon, at the close of the service, as is the custom at my church, came an invitation to discipleship. And Mr. and Mrs. Mom and Dad come down to the front. They confessed faith in Christ. Afterward, I said, 'What prompted this?' And they said, 'Well, do you know about our parties?' And I said, 'yeah, I heard about your parties.' They said, 'well, we had one last night again, and it got a little loud and it got a little rough. And there was too much drinking. And we waked our daughter, and she came downstairs, she was on the third step. And she saw that we were eating and drinking and she said, 'Oh, can I give the blessing? God is great; God is good, let us thank him for our food. Good night everybody.' She went back upstairs. 'Oh My land, it's time to go, we gotta be going. We've stayed…' Within two minutes the room was empty.' Mr. and Mrs. Mom and Dad are picking up crumpled napkins and wasted and spilled peanuts and half-sandwiches and taking empty glasses on trays to the kitchen. And with two trays he and she meet beside the sink on either side, and they look at each other, and he expresses what both are thinking, 'where do we think we're going.' The moment of truth."

In the moment of truth, there can be a new beginning. Because that's what we're here for, a new name, a new beginning. We're here to follow an itinerant preacher who wandered through town and changed the world. But half measures won't do.

We can't say, "Oh, there's a new beginning for you, but not you." We can't say, "There's grace enough for this person, but not that person." We can't say, "I'll be a Christian on Sundays, but leave my business out of this." We can't say, "I'll be a Christian unless it's unpopular or unless it's not fiscally sound," because that's not following Christ. It's an "all in" sort of thing. Peter and Andrew got up and walked away and followed Christ. They took a new beginning, and so can you. Because of the grace of God in Jesus Christ, we can all take a new beginning.

In the Name of the Father and of the Son and of the Holy Ghost, Amen.

A Little Off-the-Cuff Oenology
John 2:1-11

I was in Princeton on study leave one time when I found that my program had scheduled a lecture for my colleagues and me from Dr. Clifton Black, the seminary's new Otto Piper professor of New Testament. Any time you have a named job, that's a big deal. Dr. Black wasn't at Princeton when I was in Seminary there, so I was looking forward to hearing him and seeing what sort of direction the New Testament department is heading. I was just a touch surprised, skeptical even, when I read his lecture topic. It was Johnny Cash. You may imagine then that I was just a touch concerned about the future direction of my alma mater, but I had read about Dr. Black's work connecting the Gospel and Johnny Cash in the *Princeton Seminary Bulletin* so I decided to leave the jury out until I heard what he had to say. In the spirit of full disclosure, I'm not a huge country music fan either, so the prospects seemed just a touch bleak, to say the least.

I sat in the lecture room listening, more than a little surprised – sheepish even – to realize that I found the lecture and the music, well, toe-tapping. I decided after the lecture to expand my horizons just a bit, and hopped in my car and drove down Quakerbridge Road over to the local Best Buy (this was before iTunes) to pick up the Live at Folsom Prison album, because, and I'm slightly surprised to admit this, I liked the Folsom Prison Blues.

It seems my colleagues had beaten me to the punch, though, and all of the Live from Folsom Prison Albums had already been bought. So I settled instead on the Johnny Cash at San Quentin album, tearing the cellophane off as I walked back to my car. I quickly scanned ahead to Folsom Prison Blues and left the CD playing as I drove back to campus. As the album continued playing, there was a lengthy portion of narration by Johnny Cash between the songs, and after *Ring of Fire*, Cash decided to turn his concert in a slightly more spiritual direction and began to tell the assembled prisoners about a trip that he and his wife, June Carter Cash had taken the previous May.

Cash and Carter had taken a trip to Israel with a tape recorder to capture the sounds of the people and places of Israel. They went to Nazareth and Tiberias, capturing the sounds to share with the prisoners of San Quentin. They went to a little town called Cana, just over the hills from Nazareth, and went into a church built over the cistern where Cash informed the prisoners that the water for miracle of the wedding in Cana of Galilee was drawn. Cash said they recorded the sounds of the water splashing in the cistern, echoing in the church. He walked out of the church murmuring, "He turned the water into wine, of all things." And then he said he had the closest thing to an inspiration he ever had. In the car on the way to Tiberias, he wrote a song about the experience.

In his incomparable bass, Cash sang, "He turned the water into wine. In the little Cana town, the word went all around, he turned the water into wine."

Naturally, when I began to consider our text for this day, the wedding in Cana of Galilee, my mind raced back to the Johnny Cash album, and my cerebral jukebox began to play *He turned the water into wine* over and over and over. Continuous loop.

I've done a fair amount of reading on this passage, scholars have weighed in a fair amount on it. Raymond Brown writes of this story that there is not a paucity of symbolism, but rather an embarrassment of riches contained within it for those who would look. And through Brown's brief glance at the history of interpretation related to this story, there have been quite a number of hypothetical observations levied at this text, the most fascinating having to do, I consider, with the mathematical calculation of exactly how much wine Jesus made in his foray into a little off-the-cuff oenology. (Conservatively estimated at a hundred gallons, for inquiring minds that want to know.)

But when the academic dust settles, the point of the story remains, really, that he turned the water into wine.

John's Gospel narrative is distinctively organized into a predictable pattern, I've told you, and it's pretty easy to spot when you are reading your Bibles if you know to look for it. If you take off the very beginning and the very end, which form sort of a theological prologue and a redemptive epilogue, the intervening chapters are divided into two subcategories, or "books". There is the book of signs and the book of glory. I've talked about this before, so those of you who are familiar with John's structure, just bear with me while we review this. The first portion is the book of signs, and about halfway through, we move into the book of glory. Jesus performs signs, wonders, miracles in order that people might know who he is. The signs point to the coming glory. That's the basic idea: Signs, Glory. It's a macrocosm of the individual stories we encounter: *he turned the water into wine. In the little Cana town, the word went all around: he turned the water into wine.*

Cash is perhaps more of a Biblical interpreter than he planned to be, though, in penning this song, because he goes on to do almost exactly what the Gospel writer John did, to tell stories about Jesus and the signs he wrought in order that people might draw some conclusions about who he must be. *He fed the hungry multitudes…he walked on the sea of Galilee…*These stories do same thing: they use these signs to point to who Jesus is. Of course the way John tells the stories about Jesus, the details he chooses to include, all tell us something about who John believes that Jesus is. There is some scholarly dispute about how this particular story came to be in John and nowhere else, but in the end, in the end, the point of the story remains: *he turned the water into wine.*

So what does it matter whether or not Jesus was able to upgrade the festivities at what was probably a distant cousin's wedding? Why do we care if there was or was not a miracle that saved the host of a party from potential embarrassment? I haven't seen any signs lately that would cause me to cast my lot with John in sitting back and recounting the stories of Jesus that tell us about who he is, and perhaps more trying, tell us about who he wants us to be.

Sometimes an image becomes associated with a particular text, sometimes a preacher captures a turn of phrase that recasts a story in such a way that bridges a couple of millennia of understanding so that we, those of us trying to know who Jesus is so that we can know how Jesus wants us to live can learn something from it. Several years ago, it came in vogue to preach about this text from the standpoint of when the wine runs out. As I was reading, I came across a Baptist preacher who was here in Atlanta, a Dr. William Ireland, who looked at this text and realized that if we think about it long enough, consider what our lives look like, what's going on now, for you and me, down the street for our neighbors, sooner or later, the wine runs out for all of us. In his sermon entitled *When the Wine Gives Out*, Dr. Ireland wrote,

"It happens to all of us. The wine gives out, and what is meant to be a joyous celebration soon turns quiet, anxious and empty. Whatever we have relied on to lend order, significance, and joy to our days suddenly runs out or proves woefully inadequate. That's why we need to pay attention to what Jesus did here. He commanded the servants to take six stone water pots used for the cleaning of utensils and the washing of hands, and to fill the jars with water, right up to the brim. He then commanded that some be drawn out and taken to the steward or the headwaiter. When this man took a sip, it was not water, but fine wine. Water had become wine."

What's the significance of this? Jesus' turning water into wine is itself a picture of all that he came to do. Jesus took what is and said it has the possibility to become something else. What is can become something else. Just what you have on hand can be the main ingredient in the chemistry experiment he wants to work in your life. What is – whatever is tired, worn out, devoid of joy, empty and lacking in purpose – can be turned into something else. Something rich, fragrant, and ripe with the fullness of joy. What is, no matter how lifeless and stagnant, can be turned into something else by the power of Jesus."[1]

Do you see that? Do you see that what Jesus did thousands of years ago still has the power to turn water into wine today?

Let me ask that another way...are you tired enough, old enough, worried enough, sick enough, scared enough to be ready to think the wine has given out?

Or maybe not. Maybe just the boredom – mediocrity of it all – is getting to you. Life isn't miserable, nothings terribly wrong, it just isn't joyful. Is that where you are today? Has the wine been cheap for a long time...adequate enough, but not just not really lighting your fire. Kind of like a jug wine, a little vinegary, tastes like the plastic, plastic world.

He turned the water into wine. Of course, I can't prove that. But it's what the Bible says. It's who John says that Jesus was...concerned with life, and joy, beauty, and happiness...

Life, joy, beauty, happiness...do you know that is what Christian faith is concerned with? Do you know that is what God wants for us? I know it may come across as something of a stretch at times...another of my favorite quotes is that Presbyterianism, which I might add, I love, Presbyterianism can be defined as the nagging, horrible fear that somebody, somewhere, is having a good time. That's not the faith we are called to.

Life, joy, beauty, happiness...That's what God made us for, wants for us. That church has come to be associated with deprivation, dourness – a general lack of fun represents a lack of imagination on the part of some Christians, but it doesn't represent a lack of grace on the part of the Gospel. There was a wedding in Cana of Galilee, and Jesus turned the water into wine. There is work to be done by Christians to share this good news with the whole world that craves, needs, seeks joy and happiness, but the work doesn't diminish the joyfulness of it all.

Now, about that hundred gallons of wine. That's a conservative estimate. Some scholars do the math and land on about a hundred and fifty. I'm not

---

[1] William Ireland. *When the Wine Gives Out* in *The Library of Distinctive Sermons.* p 283

sufficiently versed in ancient weights and measurements to throw my two cents in on whether it was a hundred or a hundred and fifty, but here's the kicker: it was a lot of wine. Wine makes me light up like a Christmas tree but I still enjoy it and in the corner of my breakfast room, because it's out of direct sunlight where I store the bottles that I have bought for myself and that others have bought for me. When that cabinet is full, I think it holds in the order of oh, say, twenty-five bottles. (I didn't go count.) That's maybe four or five gallons of wine. A bottle holds 750ml, and that isn't much wine. The point of all this math is that a hundred, or a hundred and fifty: it's a lot of wine. It's a cellar full. It's at least 250 bottles of wine. In fact, one of the more fanciful interpretations that I encountered on this passage had to do with the fact that Jesus produced a hundred gallons of wine. I think the preacher disapproved.

But that is the point! Grace, goodness, happiness, joy – it's overflowing. It's more than is needed. It's the life abundant that Jesus promised.

Poet Laureate Richard Wilbur writes:

St. John tells how, at Cana's wedding feast/ the water pots poured wine in such amount/ that by his sober count/ there were a hundred gallons at the least.

It made no earthly sense, unless to show/ how whatsoever love elects to bless/ brims to sweet excess/ that can without depletion overflow.

Which is to say that what love sees is true/ that the world's fullness is not made but found/ life hungers not to abound/ and pour its plenty out for such as you.[2]

But isn't that the point! He changed the water into wine!

If you are wondering if that is, in fact, the point of the sermon, well yes, it is. But we're not counting so much on believing that Christ did it so long ago as we're counting on recognizing that he did it yesterday. Or the day before. Or hoping that he is going to do it tomorrow. Because he can. Because he will.

I know the wine gives out sometimes. It'll give out for me, and for you, and from time to time these elders and deacons will feel it. But the Gospel is about new life – life overflowing, blessing from God.

---

[2] Richard Willard. *A Wedding Toast* in *Divine Inspiration: The Life of Jesus in Poetry*. p 113

The thing about blessings is that we can't really predict them. When we receive them they don't tell us so much when they are coming again. And perhaps most frustrating of all, blessings sometimes take a while to identify themselves as such. Or maybe, rather, it takes a while for God to bring a blessing out of some things.

But the Gospel does promise that we will have life abundant and that it will exceed what we can possibly consider imagining.

I sure wish I could tell you for sure what it's going to look like. I can't. You can't. I can only tell you he turned the water into wine. At least the Bible tells me so.

I want to tell you that he is going to turn the water into wine again. And I believe that he is. But I don't want to cheapen that wine, or turn it into some sort of brew-thru, where we claim in useless discipleship that God's going to bless us and give no thought to how God is going to use us to bless others.

And I'm not going to cheapen God's blessings by telling you the wine will never run dry again. It will, for you, and for me. For all of us some day the wine stops running.

Wherever you are when the wine runs dry, just remember, he turned the water into wine.

In the name of the Father, and of the Son, and of the Holy Ghost, Amen.

A New Zoo
Isaiah 11:1-10; Romans 15:4-13

I was visiting my friend Sherri in Philadelphia one time when it became clear very quickly that the plans that we had for the day were going to change when her twin niece and nephew were added into the mix.

Knowing that they would be less than interested in brunch at the latest boutique gastro pub, we quickly abandoned our plans and changed course.

Sherri is an animal lover. When she's not busy with her day job as a Presbyterian Minister, she volunteers at local animal rehab facilities. She has handled raptors and seals and other things that I only view through windows or on screens. I sort of limit it to dogs and cats myself, and the occasional odd bird. Seriously, when the preschool had reptile day last fall I declined to come by the church until it was declared a snake-free zone.

So of course, I kept my lips buttoned when Sherri and her brother determined that the Philadelphia Zoo would be a great way to keep the children occupied and entertained.

The truth is, though, I don't really like zoos. I don't like seeing animals removed from the wild. Frankly, I have a hard time even reconciling myself with crating my dogs when I'm not home, and that is done for the good of greater Decatur.

I did a good job of keep my mouth shut until we got to the large cats and the lion came out onto a bluff overlooking the lionesses and let out an anemic sounding roar.

"Oh, you king of beasts," I said, "To what an ignominious place you've come."

Sherri turned to me and said, "Speaking of beasts, you might want to climb down off that high horse before you fall. That lion was born in captivity. He would last one week on the savannah. If he's going to live, this is where it's going to be. Zoos aren't like they were in the old days, this is an educational institution."

Of course, she's right.

A few years later we were in Scotland, just north of Oban, on our way to Iona where I was going to spend some time doing nothing and she was going to do some ongoing research into the place of wildlife in Celtic Spirituality, and she told me, "There's a Sea Lion Sanctuary on the way, I'd really like to stop and see what they're doing."

So again, my anti-zoo sentiment reared its head. "Sherri, I don't really want to look at a bunch of poor sea lions swimming around in circles in some tepid puddle for the amusement of anyone who happened to pull off the motorway."

And again, I was foiled, "It's a rescue sanctuary," she said, "the injured pups are brought here and fed until the come up to weight and then they are released back into the wild. They've been tracking them for years and they have a ninety percent success rate. It's not a zoo. If anything, it's a new kind of zoo."

I thought about that this week as I considered Isaiah's zoo because in each instance the reality was completely different from what I expected.

That is the heart of Isaiah's vision – that nothing is as it seems. Nothing is the way we expect it to be.

That is, of course, the magic of Isaiah's vision – that nothing is as we expect it to be.

Lions and lambs don't hang out together. Not for long, at least. Same with leopards and kids – you *can* put them together but expect some nice gloves at the end of the day.

I've never seen a grazing bear.

And we all know where I am when there are snakes in the building.

Maybe you remember that wonderful Edward Hicks folk painting that hangs in the national gallery… it's called *The Peaceable Kingdom*, and it is this text come to life… there is a possum like-bear hanging out next to a cow gnawing on some straw, there is another cow next to a regal, restrained, elegantly serene lion, and in the midst is a toddler.

We don't put toddlers in the middle of the zoo enclosures either, come to think of it.

The whole thing looks like a farce.

Isaiah's listeners would have thought it was farcical too.

Most of us think of prophecy and assume that it is a prognostication – a looking ahead to some sort of distant future – we hear Isaiah and we think of Jesus, who of course, is many hundreds of years into the future from when Isaiah was preaching.

The reality is, though, that Isaiah was preaching a present word for a present reality. Whatever we think that Isaiah has to say about Jesus, he starts with a word to his people about their situation right then.

It is useful to think of Isaiah as having about three periods for what he had to say. There's *before the invasion, during the invasion,* and *after the invasion.* These three periods spread over a long period of time, and through it all, people writing under the guise of Isaiah bring a word from God.

First it is a word of warning.

It is long and verbose but at its heart it is quite a simple warning to the people: *if you stay on this path, there will be consequences.*

The path of course is placing their trust, as a people, elsewhere from God.

Then it is a word of resignation: *the consequences have come; now we are living with them.*

And finally, it is a word of promise: *God will return us to our homes. This time in exile will not last forever.*

What I find so wonderful about Isaiah, though, is this: in every age of the prophecy, whether it is warning, or resignation, or even in the end looking to an eventual promise, there remains throughout the element of *hope.*

Our reading this morning, the absurd vision of the peaceable kingdom wherein logic is stood on its head with unpredictable animal behavior, is just such a word of hope.

It begins simply enough. A root shall come out of the stump of Jesse…

In the scenes before we read this, Isaiah warns of the utter deforestation of Israel. All that is living will be cut down, thrown as fuel into the fire.

If you stay on this path, there will be consequences, and they will be bad, is the warning of Isaiah.

But... there is hope, even in hopeless circumstances.

Even in the midst of rampant destruction and the promise of more to come, there is a line that hearkens back to better days.

A root shall come out of the stump of Jesse.

David was Jesse's son.

David was Israel's high water mark.

David was the king against whom all other kings were measured.

David was the king who was after God's own heart, the king, both gifted and flawed, who sinned before the Lord and also confessed his sin, whose trust remained in the God who sustained him, and whose trust formed the heart of God's covenant with Israel.

We read it and we may race ahead to Jesus, but those listeners of Isaiah's word would have raced back to David, back to the promise, back to the other reality – that God is not done with them yet.

All that we see may present one reality – but God has a different vision sometimes. God has a different vision – perhaps all the time.

I read this week of a recording that was made by Simon and Garfunkel in the 1960's.

It was an art piece, designed to make a point. They recorded the hymn *Silent Night* against the backdrop of the Vietnam War. Against the strains of the song were heard the staccato punctuation of gunshots.[3]

The point is clear. The specter of war slashes at the salvific strains of the hymn. The reality of war and death negates the warm glow of candlelight around the carol reducing it to a fairy-tale.

But I wonder if there is another way to hear it?

---

[3] *Pulpit Digest*, Nov-Dec 1990. p 19

What if we reverse the way we listen to it?

What if the strains of the carols wash over the ugliness of gunshots, presenting instead a new vision -their vision of a coming world?

Of course, it's true of every age.

Every issue of *The Week* magazine has a section that is titled, "The US at a glance..."

It's a recap of this past week's news. There were six entries this week, let me tell you what they were. Three white San Jose State students were accused of hate crimes for decorating a dorm with Confederate flags, forcing their black roommate to wear a bicycle lock around his neck and calling him, 'three fifths' in a reference to the US Constitution recognizing slaves as three-fifths of a person. In New York City, a pandemic of attacks are attributed to adolescents playing what is called "the knockout game" in which an unsuspecting stranger is punched in the back of the head. The teen wins the game if the victim is knocked out in a single glow. In Boston, a crime lab technician was sentenced to three to five years in jail for falsifying records leading to hundreds of convictions and burnishing her career. In Steubenville, Ohio, a grand jury indicted four school employees for covering up the rape of 16-year-old in 2012. In Birmingham, a posthumous pardon was granted to three black men 82 years after they were falsely accused of a crime, convicted by all-white juries in 1931. And in Newtown, Connecticut, the Lanza Report was released.[4]

It's not always that bad, but what a week!

I don't know about you, but I need a new zoo.

I need a different vision of reality.

I need redemption.

I need the hymns and carols to play over this and tell their stories of redemption.

The heart of the Gospel is the story of redemption.

---

[4] *The Week*, Dec. 6, 2013. p 7

The whole Bible is the story of hope.

That's why the hope springs through in Isaiah – because God is never done.

Walter Brueggemann writes,

"The Old Testament voices the oldest, deepest, most resilient grounding of hope in all of human history…

YHWH has sworn to effect futures of well-being that are beyond the present condition of the world and that cannot, in any credible way, be extrapolated from the present."[5]

That is the hope of the Gospel: that when it appears that things are just about as bad as they could possibly be – when things are as bad as a messiah strung up on a cross – that God is not done, that God is never done, that we can yet hear "the clear, though far off strains that hail a new creation…"

That is the Gospel promise: that hope never dries up. That God can, and God will, create a new reality, a vision as absurd as a peaceable kingdom.

You know, for most of us, when your life is going great, then there's probably not so much for me to say to you today about a hopeful future. But maybe for one or two – or may three or four of us, life is hard and loneliness creeps in. Maybe for a handful of us – or perhaps more than a handful – Christmas is just one more expense, one more looming pressure needing quickly to pass. Or maybe you are mourning. Holidays are hard when you're mourning; I think perhaps the hardest of all.

Don't give up, there's a new zoo coming, and God has plans.

From the shreds of what could have been, God puts together a new creation, again and again.

That is what redemption is. It is God taking what *is* and making it into what *can be*.

I love a story that Anne Lamott tells in her new book, Stitches.

After her dog, Bodhi, shredded two different sets of curtains defending her against an unknown threat, either an assassin or the postman, she was left

---

[5] Walter Brueggemann. *Reverberations of Faith.* (Westminster/JKP: Louisville, 2002) p 100

with two curtains that were perfectly fine in the upper portions, but ripped to pieces in the lower portions as her dog leapt through them, ultimately wearing them, much like the tutu wearing hippos of *Fantasia*.

She writes that she gave them to her friend to see what could be made from them. Two tops of curtains, no bottoms, and a seamstress. She writes,

"She wondered if the two tops could be mated, and ended up taking them home to see what she could do. This is all restoration requires most of the time, that one person not give up."

After telling the story of her friend's creative work, she concludes, "The newly sewn curtain was fabulous and crazy. Whereas before it had been logical and tranquil, now it was one wild lake of designs. Once it was two torn up curtains, and now it was a whole, although a whole with issues… beauty is a miracle of things going together imperfectly… what might have been thrown out went from tattered scraps to something majestic and goofy and honest that holds together, that keeps people's eyes off of me and my family, yet lets in light and sun, like a poem or a song.

You have to keep taking the next necessary stitch, and the next one, and the next.

Without stitches, you just have rags.

And we are not rags."[6]

In the name of the Father, and of the Son and of the Holy Ghost, Amen.

---

[6] Anne Lamott. *Stitches: A Handbook on Meaning, Hope and Repair.* (Riverhead, NY 2013) pp 82-83.

Into the Far Country
Luke 15:11-32

A colleague of mine was writing a sermon series on the parables of Jesus and he had almost decided to leave out the story of the prodigal son. "Too overexposed," he thought. "We're too familiar with it, it has lost its shock value in our culture." After he thought of it, he decided that he would be pilloried if he preached a series on the parables and omitted this one, so he chickened out, and preached the sermon.

Another colleague, Tom Tewell, has made the declaration that if he had only one chapter of the Bible to share the essential good news, he would pick Luke 15.

Still another colleague, writing for preachers, cautioned: don't explain this story. People know what it means. Parsing it out would have all the awkwardness of an explained joke. Let the story do its work, he advises.

The Prodigal Son story is a favorite. Why? What about it speaks to us so deeply? Without belaboring the story, I'd like to take a crack at it again today because I believe all of my colleagues are right. It is overexposed; and yet it is the Gospel.

You know the characters; I don't need to describe them to you again. But this might bear repeating: you *know* these characters. You *know* the good guys and the bad guys. You *know* the people who won't be bothered to care about anyone but themselves. You *know* the old softie.

Moreover, we identify with the characters; that's why the story works. We can readily identify with the son who stayed home and did what he was told and seethed while his profligate younger brother got paved a highway with his parents and all the bad things were swept away when he came traipsing home. I, for one, can identify with the younger brother. My older brother is an emergency physician. No one ever created a TV show about the emergency work of the minister! So I get it when he finally cracks and says, "you know what, let me make my way. I might fail, but at least it's *my way*." And then of course, there is the beleaguered parent, affronted by the younger son, harangued by the older, he stands in the middle and says, "can't we all just get along?"

Oh, you know them. You may *be* them! They need no explanation. But they do bear repetition. My colleague was worried they would become too commonplace, too ordinary. They've lost their scandal because we've heard the story so many times.

Well, I suppose we have heard the story plenty of times. Henri Nouwen wrote a classic book, *The Return of the Prodigal Son*, based on the classic Rembrandt painting, *The Return of the Prodigal Son*. We've heard the story – it appears in art and literature. Repetition could make it commonplace.

But you know, grace should be commonplace! I'm not convinced that making something commonplace means we render it irrelevant.

No. Taking something into our being, making it a part of who we are is NOT making it ordinary or common. I don't think this story loses its power because we've heard it before. It gains power precisely because we've heard it before. Here's your PSA for the day: if you want your Bible to have power, read it.

This story is plenty scandalous no matter how often we read it, because it is a story about grace, and grace is scandalous at its heart.

In some ways, I suppose that is the point of the story. That is why my colleague would pick Luke 15 as the synopsis of the Gospel if he had to – because it is a ringing affirmation that grace is never, ever ordinary, but it nevertheless abounds.

I've told you my working definition of grace: Grace is the undeserved, unmerited, unconditional love of God.

It should never become something to be taken for granted. That's what Bonhoeffer meant when he cautioned Christians against believing in and relying on cheap grace. Cheap grace is where we've become so familiar with the story, so blasé about it, that we actually begin to believe that, because God has done it all, what we do doesn't matter.

In the ancient church that was called anti-nomianism and it was ruled a heresy, with good reason. What we do *does* matter.

In our Presbyterian, reformed tradition, we are so gun-shy about works righteousness that we have almost come full circle right back around to anti-nomianism. We are so worried about salvation and making sure that we don't make it a work that we humans have to do on our own behalves that we have very nearly rendered grace meaningless by our inaction.

What we do *does* matter. To think otherwise is to believe in a cheap grace. God has done everything for our salvation. Grace is real: it is unconditional, undeserved and unmerited. But if grace is to have any transformative power in our lives, we have to acknowledge that our actions – and our inaction – matter.

This story is scandalous precisely because it points us to this very demanding reality: God has called us to the reconciliation of the world, and we may do so precisely because grace *is* commonplace.

What we do does matter. The actions of the young man did yield consequences. You know the story. He wandered off into the far country and squandered it all in dissolute living. Take your pick for what that means. The legacy of our Victorian and Puritan forbears would leave us assuming that means sex and liquor, hard drugs if you're really feeling saucy. But it could have been anything. In many ways that is the beauty of the text. *It could have been anything…* we don't know what went wrong. Let me ask you: have you ever had that shot at and missed feeling?

Have you ever realized that, "Well, it turned out okay this time, but it could have gone so very differently?"

If you have ever had the sickening realization that it could have gone the other way, you have a point of entry into this text.

Or, perhaps you *have* hit bottom. You do know what the end of the road looks like. You've been there. You've know the marriage can't be saved and shouldn't be. You've woken up after the bender and thought, "I'm going to die if I keep this up…" You've felt the judgment weighing on you because each move you made to correct a previous move went wrong and the business failed and your family is going to have to pick up the slack.

If you know what it is to have averted a disaster or have experienced one and had to clean up after it, then you probably know the power of grace… you have a point of entry into the text, into the power of the unconditional love of God, the undeserved, unmerited inbreaking of kindness.

The text says that no one gave him anything.

Scholars hypothesize that the pods in question were carob pods which lack any real nutritional value, won't do anything for you but make you feel full, and he would have gladly filled himself on them, *but no one gave him anything.*

That ought to bother us in a story about grace. *No one gave him anything.*

There's something about that far country. It's an inhospitable place. We're to understand that it has some clear allure for the young man… we're to understand by extension that the far country has some repulsive allure for us if we are to take any meaning from this story.

In the far country, you are apparently on your own. In the far country, if you fall, there's no safety net. "You can sleep with the pigs, but don't touch their food; we need them fat for harvest." He would have eaten the pods, but nobody gave him anything.

I don't want to live in the far country. How about you?

I'm not sure we have to go very far to find the far country. We won't go there, but we could, and it's a long way off, but it's not a far journey.

Do you know where the far country is? It's in rural Appalachia and inner-city Atlanta. It's in country clubs and brothels.

If you know where to look, you'll see it. We have a mission team in New Orleans right now, and I bet they've seen some far country. We have volunteers who work in food co-ops and fix meals for shelters because they know there is some far country not very far away. If you need to know the directions to the far country, ask our deacons, I bet maybe they can tell you.

Nobody wants to go to the far country. We all know it is out there, but what troubles me about that far country, is that *nobody gave him anything.*

The text tells us he came to himself.

I don't know just what that means. Some folks interpret it graciously: the son recognized the error of his ways, knew he had done bad, wanted nothing more than to go home and have someone care about him again.

Others are more skeptical, more cynical: he came to his senses. He realized he's starving to death. Just come up with a good speech, hit the road! Get on home where even the servants have a better deal, and on the road come up with a good cover story, con the old man, he always had a blind spot, didn't he?

You know the rest of the story. He goes home, he gets spotted across the field, his geriatric father hikes up his skirt and takes off running for him and it is a picture of grace: new robe, new ring, big feast.

And then… and then, the far country comes home. No one would give him anything.

There's that older son. Truly he has done everything right. He went to school. He paid his bills. He never asked for anything. All he ever did was do right, stay home, take care of the parental units… and suddenly, there we are in the far country again… no one gave him anything.

"I have worked for you," he said, "I have slaved, and you never threw me a party."

Oh, the far country is a lonely place.

Did you know that you can get it all right and still wind up in the far country?

Did you know that you can play by all the rules and work hard and still wind up in the far country? Did you know that you can do all the right things and one day, one day, your job's gone overseas, and there you are in the far country?

Did you know that you can work so hard at a marriage you don't think you've got anything else to give to and, one day, one day, your spouse comes home and says there's nothing left, and there you are, off in the far country.

Who am I asking? You all know this. You know the far country can be a moving target.

That is what is so poignant about this story: everyone knows what it is to hurt. Everyone knows that you can gamble and lose, and there you are, far country. Everyone knows that one day your children grow up and they don't need you like they once did. Far country. Everyone knows what it is to be underappreciated, to work, work, work and have someone else get the party. Far country.

Karl Barth took this story and turned it on its head when he made the claim that Jesus is the son who went into the far country for us. Jesus is the one who, in a world "where no one would give him anything," gave everything, enduring the sin, isolation and pain of journeying into the far country for us.

Perhaps you saw that movie, "What Dreams May Come" a number of years ago. It takes place in a fictitious afterlife. Robin Williams, a physician who was killed in a car accident shortly after the death of his children, is reunited with them in a heavenly playground, colorful and bright. In time, he realizes something is horribly wrong. His wife is missing. Bereft of her husband and children, she ends her life.

The result of her tragic death is to plunge her into terror and blackness and fear. Believing that nothing can be right if this is left so, Williams' character plunges himself into the very same terror, darkness and fear to go after her. In his dogged pursuance of her, he reminds her of joy, reminds her to cling to joy, and thus pulls her back into the light, into color and playfulness and joy.

That is the essence of Jesus' journey into the far country. He came to pull us, all of us, back from the world of darkness and fear and terror into the world of color and light and joy. Into a world, "where no one would give him anything," the son journeyed into the far country to bring us out.

We are everyone in this story. We are eldest son and youngest. We are waiting father and mother. For all of these, and for all of us, Jesus went into the far country so that the world where "no one gave him anything," could be transformed.

That is why ultimately, this is a story of great joy. There is joy in heaven. There is joy on earth because the darkness did not win.

You see, that's the promise we make when we baptize. You do remember we baptize children of God of every age, and when we baptize we make them a promise: we promise that we will go with them even to the far country, because that is where Jesus found us, because this is a story about grace.

In the name of the Father, and of the Son, and of the Holy Ghost, Amen.

From Where Will My Help Come?
Psalm 121; Romans 4:1-5, 13-17

I remember it like it was yesterday. A young woman in the congregation I was serving scheduled lunch with me but asked for ten minutes in my office beforehand. That wasn't surprising, we were working together on a project and we were good friends. I had baptized her children, counseled with her when her mother became ill; we served alongside one another in Christian Education committee meetings – that was before we call it Children's ministry or Adult Faith development. She was and still is someone I found easy to talk to, easy to work with, friendly to be around – but willing to engage her faith with her church family and with me. Nonetheless, I was surprised by the request for ten minutes of office time before the working lunch.

As she came into my office, we settled into the comfortable chairs in the "visiting" part of my office, and I expected that we would have a conversation like we always did – about church work, our families – I was expecting a familiar conversation.

It wasn't.

"I can't pray anymore," she said.

I was taken aback. "Tell me more."

"That's just it. I can't pray anymore. It's lost its meaning. I'm not inspired to it. I mean, I just don't have any words for what I'm feeling – frankly, I feel lost."

I was floored. I had no inkling of an impending faith crisis.

"Do you have any idea why?" I asked.

"Yes," she said, "I could go through a laundry list with you of what is stressing me out, but I'm not inclined to, and before you ask, yes, I already have a therapist and my dosage is correct. I'm just not able to pray."

We sat there for a few minutes with the silence between us. She, waiting. Me, collecting my thoughts.

She broke the silence, "I don't know what I expect you to say, maybe there's nothing to say…"

I interrupted her, "No, I – I do have something. What is your favorite Psalm?"

"121."

"That is one of my favorites too. Could you pray it?"

"You mean read it instead of praying?"

"No," I said, "Can you read it in place of trying to come up with your own words. Read it as your prayer. Read it for the people you want to pray for, substitute their names for the pronouns. Read it as many times as you need to pray."

"Of course, I can read it, but isn't that going to get old quickly?"

"Was what you *were* doing feeling particularly fresh to you?" (We had that kind of friendship.) With that, we left to get lunch.

A week or so later, I asked her how it was going.

She laughed, "Well, between praying the 121st Psalm for myself and for each member of my family, I've been reading it about 5 times a day – and I've memorized it. I don't need the Bible; I can just launch into it anytime I feel like it." And then she chuckled, "I have also been using it defensively."

"Meaning…"
"I caught myself the other day when my daughter was being particularly obnoxious asking for her lunch… I prayed, 'Lift up her eyes to the hills Lord, from whence cometh her peanut butter and jelly. Her peanut butter and jelly cometh from the mom, the maker of pizza rolls and hot dogs."

"Are you sure your dosage doesn't need an adjustment?"

Amidst the laughter, she said, "It is working, you know. I needed prayer that was grounded in something with a little more substance and gravitas than what my own words could come up with. It did work. It is working."

There are those times in life when we need something that is grounded in a little more substance and gravitas than what we can generate from within ourselves. In a sound byte world, words that have the ring of eternity about them have a way of reducing everything around them to two dimensions – white noise if you will.

Certain words can cut through the clichés.

Some words have a way of compounding upon themselves the more often they are heard. That is why we incorporate a certain amount of repetition into the order of worship. I hope you've noticed after all these years that we use the Psalms to prepare ourselves to worship each week, and we use the Pauline hymns of grace for our assurance of pardon most weeks – it's because it's possible to go months, years, and never hear those words if we don't hear them in worship, but they are words we need to hear:

My help is in the Lord, the maker of heaven and earth.

I don't know that I believe faith needs to be hard – Jesus said, after all, that his yoke was easy and his burden was light – and of course he was talking about the very rules of the temple establishment – the Law – that Paul tells us was not imputed to Abraham as righteousness – and then Paul goes on and says that it is Abraham's trust that God saw as righteous. "Abraham believed God," he writes.

That's trust.

Sometimes it is hard to maintain that trust. We need the words we know not to fail us then. That's when we don't want to be fumbling in a book to find them. We want them written deep, deep within us.

That's the sort of faith that can't come overnight. It's not characterized by hot emotion or short-term inspiration, it is grounded and rooted faith. It is faith that has matured by means of a long obedience in the same direction.

When they are written deep within us, the words themselves become foundational. They're the building blocks of faith to be sure, but they're more. They're what we come back to.

Sometimes we *need* to come back to what matters.

Fred Craddock tells a great story of visiting a member of the congregation in the hospital. This person had never had surgery before and was scared out of her wits. So Craddock went to the hospital to visit and he said he looked around the hospital room and there were magazines and books stacked up – and it was all the sort of stuff you or I might read on the beach or in the dentist's office. There were magazines like Us Weekly (one of my colleagues calls it US Weekly so it sounds like a news magazine. People. (I shove that one inside a copy of National Geographic while I'm waiting to get my teeth cleaned so that my fellow patients won't judge me.)

Anyway, it was that sort of stuff, which is of course all perfectly fine to read. And Craddock looked at the whole stack of books and magazines and thought, "there's not a calorie in that whole stack to help her through her experience. She had no place to dip down in to a reservoir and come up with something – a word, a phrase, a thought, an idea, a memory, a person. Just empty.

How marvelous is the life of someone who, like a wise homemaker, when the berries and fruits of and vegetables are ripe, puts them away in jars and cans in the cellar. Then when the ground is cold, icy and barren, and nothing seems alive, she goes down into the cellar, comes up, and it's May and June at her family's table. How blessed is that person."[7]

I know that story's a little old, and the language might be a little sexist, but there's truth to it, isn't there?

I lift up my eyes to the hills -- from where will my help come?

My help comes from the LORD, who made heaven and earth.

He will not let your foot be moved; he who keeps you will not slumber.

He who keeps Israel will neither slumber nor sleep.

The LORD is your keeper; the LORD is your shade at your right hand.

The sun shall not strike you by day, nor the moon by night.

The LORD will keep you from all evil; he will keep your life.

The LORD will keep your going out and your coming in from this time on and forevermore.

Don't you just *love* that? I love that. And I don't know if I love it because I've heard it for years and years or because when I hear it the strains of Mendelsohn are playing in the background or just because it spoke to me one day and caught my heartstring and held it.

---

[7] Fred Craddock, *Craddock Stories*, Graves and Ward, eds. (Chalice Press: St. Louis, 2001) p 30

I don't know.

But I do know this: even after more than four decades of listening to it, even after preaching on it for years, I was surprised with a fresh take on this text as I considered it this week.

I've always told you that the Psalter – that's just the book of Psalms by the way – the Psalter is the hymnal of Ancient Israel. These are the songs they wrote as they were formed by hardship into an even more cohesive body.

You know suffering together does that. I don't recommend it as a means of community building, but nothing pushes any group together faster than holding up in the face of shared hardship – it either tears you up or builds you up – or maybe it just exposes what's underneath, but for the ancient Israelites in slavery in a foreign land, it built them up. And they wrote the Psalms. They're the songs they sang to each other in hardship.

Anyway, one scholar of the Psalms that I read wrote that there is good evidence to believe that this particular psalm would have been shared as a responsive litany.

James Mays notes that it can serve as the song of approach to Jerusalem as the pilgrim's eyes are lifted up to see the distant hills surrounding the holy city. The power of that image is that it is sung between friends who dream of a far-off day when they will return to the place that they love.

And what I love most of all about the idea of this Psalm as a litany is the thought that we might sing it back and forth to one another as a means of encouragement – as a means of reminding each other of our baptisms – that God has promised to be with us always, even to the end of the age, that there is more love in God than there is sin in us, that grace always wins, and love never dies. All of those words of faith, slowly internalized, slowly imbued with meaning, year in and year out, sort of like the Psalm, singing back and forth to one another just like we promised at baptism.

Praying the psalm, singing it, repeating it – it's a means of looking from the position of hardship to that more hopeful future. Again, as I was considering the text this week, I pulled yet another book off the shelf, an old friend's familiar handwriting was on the bottom of the page. Like the opening words of a litany, she wrote, "The movement of faith is from orientation to disorientation to reorientation. The two moves are what faith is all about – to embrace suffering, a characteristically Jewish move, theologically significant as an act of hope – to move into the new orientation. Hope is the Jewish gift to the world."

And just under the word, "disorientation," she wrote, "Sometimes we get a lot of mileage out of this."

There are words that reorient us. There are words that help us get our right bearing in the world. There are words that help us shake loose of whatever mileage we might be getting out of staying stuck in a place of despondency by simply singing the words of hope.

I lift up my eyes to the hills, from where will my help come? My help is in the LORD, the maker of Heaven and Earth.

In the Name of the Father, and of the Son, and of the Holy Ghost, Amen.

What are Human Beings?
Psalm 8; Romans 5:1-5

Let me tell you about the origins of the "bunny rabbit policy." I know, it sounds like an episode of *The Big Bang Theory*, and it's probably just as absurd, but stay with me.

My love-hate relationship with Social Media is pretty well known. I've been up front with you all about it: I love seeing your pictures, but I hate seeing people's over-sharing and airing their dirty laundry or their political grievances. It was this last one that led to the bunny rabbit policy. I've been a little bit more forceful in recent weeks with some of the more absurd threads, but by and large this is what the bunny rabbit policy looks like: when I reach the point that I feel that I must express something – I don't. Let me explain.

Some months back – I don't even think we were even close to the primary election, I posted something relatively mild as an opinion, and one of our members here replied. Now, our politics are not the same but it doesn't matter because we're friends -between us it was a funny poke back and forth sort of light-hearted joke that you can do when you're in the same room, or the same city.

Then, a third party, a friend but not a close friend, proceeded to eviscerate the first friend.

I was nothing short of horrified. I deleted the thread and said instead, "From now on, I am not posting anything but pictures of puppy dogs, unicorns and rainbows that way there will be no more casualties in my social media."

Of course, the first response was someone objecting to rainbows.

The next was the observation that unicorns have some vaguely sexual connotation.

Finally, someone noted that I was favoring puppy dogs over kitty cats, and what did I have against cat people anyhow?

After many rounds of mock-outrage, it was decided that a bunny rabbit should be sufficiently inoffensive. I waited until the next time I saw something that was, to my mind, bone-headed and instead of commenting, I put a rabbit on it.

It felt good. I invite you to embrace this lowly cottontail in our common discourse.

It sounds silly, and of course it is, but here's the underlying reason: in that first moment when I saw someone being ugly to a friend of mine in a public venue, I was done with it. I decided then and there that there wasn't a political or personal viewpoint that I needed to share that was worth more than my friends.

That's not to say there's nothing worth fighting for, it's to say there's a way to have that fight.

When it comes to what really matters, we can express our beliefs in ways that enhance our humanity or in ways that diminish our humanity.

That is true of more than political speech and religious convictions as well.

When it comes to the way that we live in our marriages or partnerships, we can live in ways that enhance our humanity or in ways that diminish our humanity.

When it comes to how we conduct ourselves in business, we can enhance our humanity or diminish it.

Being human is God's gift to us.

I want to make sure that sinks in: being *human* is God's gift to us.

One of my theological pet-peeves is when I see humanity being diminished. That happens when humanity is used as an excuse for inhuman, or inhumane behavior. You've heard it done, I'm sure, and it typically goes like this: I'm only human.

Maybe you've said it:

"I am afraid I blew a gasket with the meter attendant from Park Atlanta. Well, you're only human."

"I can't believe we ate that whole cheesecake! Well, we're only human."

"Does God really mind if I fudge just the teensiest bit on my 1099 income? Come on, you'd have to be superhuman not to do that!"

You see where this is going?

It is the use of humanity as an excuse for bad behavior.

Our humanity isn't what makes us do bad things. Being human is what God *created* us to be.

The problem with all those examples is that they confuse being human with being a sinner.

Human beings are sinners, but that isn't what makes us human, because sin is what diminishes humanity.

I am aware that sin is an unpopular topic.

Do you remember Robert Schuller? He was a televangelist who sort of took over the mantle of Norman Vincent Peale, of *The Power of Positive Thinking* fame. I remember seeing his *Hour of Power* broadcasts from the Crystal Cathedral on television when I was a kid. Well, some years ago, I worked with a minister who knew him well, and he pointed out to me that any reference to *sin* was, particularly in the later years, edited out of the service.

What a difference from our forebears.

Cornelius Plantinga observes that our understanding of sin has certainly changed in recent years. "The awareness of sin used to be our shadow. Christians hated sin, feared it, fled from it, grieved over it. Some of our grandparents agonized over their sins. A man who lost his temper might wonder whether he could still go to Holy Communion. A woman who for years envied her more attractive and intelligent sister might worry that this sin threatened her very salvation. But the shadow has dimmed. Nowadays the accusation *you have sinned* is often said with a grin, and with a tone that signals an inside joke."[8]

Indeed, my friend Tom Long penned an article some years back that captures the heart of the matter, using the ancient confession of sin. Its title was, "Lord Be Merciful to Me, A Miscalculator."

---

[8] Cornelius Plantinga. *Not the Way It's Supposed to Be: A Breviary of Sin.* (Eerdmans: Grand Rapids, 1995) p xi

No, we do not do the thing that we wish we had not because we are human. We do it because we are sinners. It is a lamentable fact of reality, not an excuse.

To be human means to be limited, but it does not mean to be bad. Indeed, at the ancient council of Chalcedon in 451, the humanity of Jesus was lifted up as a good thing, not to be ignored or diminished but to be embraced. That Jesus Christ is fully human is to be celebrated. Indeed, the Chalcedonian formula that Jesus is fully human and fully divine embraces the reality that to be human is to be fully and completely as God created us to be. It is *good* to be human!

We misunderstand our humanity if we think it is our sin that defines us. I love the hymn *Amazing Grace*, but note that the state of wretchedness doesn't endure to the end – it is only the awareness of the author's sin that makes him a wretched

So, don't diminish your humanity!

And just so we're clear: You can only diminish your own humanity, you can't diminish anyone else's. That's one of the great gifts given out of the language of civil rights – the knowledge that what someone calls you does not define you. What you call someone doesn't define them. Humanity is defined by God, and it is given by God.

Why does our perception of our humanity matter so much? Because God sees being human as good thing.

Do you know that? I mean, do you know that at a deep level? God sees being human as a good thing! God made you to be you! God delights in the particularity of *you!*

Listen to the Psalmist: "What are human beings that you are mindful of them, mortals that you care for them? Yet you have made them a little lower than God, and crowned them with glory and honor. You have given them dominion over the works of your hands; you have put all things under their feet, all sheep and oxen, and also the beasts of the field, the birds of the air, and the fish of the sea, whatever passes along the paths of the seas."

That is what it means to be human to God. To be a little lower than God and crowned with glory and honor.

Is that how you think of yourself?

Is that how you think of the person covered in sores and bodily fluids from diseases contracted from intravenous drug use -because in God's eyes, that person is crowned with glory and honor!

God knows sin is real! Trust me when I tell you that, in fact, God does know whether fudge your 1099 income or not, and God *does* know if you're sneaking around cheating on your spouse, and God *does* know if you're getting beaten down, and God *does* know if you look in the mirror and call yourself names, and God *does* know if you cut yourself emotionally or physically, or if you hate yourself, or if somebody else is telling you things that make you think you're less than human.

God knows sin is real. But God's grace is always more real.

And even though we don't stop being sinners, God still thinks you're crowned with glory and honor, can you believe that? Why would we ever treat ourselves otherwise?

And God doesn't dismiss sin, God addresses sin.

That's the heart of the good news of the Gospel: God knew that sin was real and hurtful and so God did something about it.

To be human is to be made in the image of God. Male and female alike, according to Genesis, made in the image of God.

Classically, the language of the Trinity is *Father, Son, and Holy Ghost.* Just a note about language: the gender is not the important part, the relationship is the important part, which is why I don't use pronouns in anything I write about God. If it's a quote, like the Aaronic benediction I use, I let it stand, but otherwise I avoid the pronouns. But I still use the classical language not because I believe God has a gender identity, but because it preserves the nature of *relationship* as the quality that defines it. Creator, Redeemer and Sustainer reflect activities. But familial language reflects relationship, and we are baptized into that relationship. God's definition of self is mutual, relational, and loving. That is who God is, and God made us in God's image.

And then, out of the overflowing of God's love, God made creation and put us in it, to be together, crowned with glory and honor.

And of course, you know the story: We mucked it up, and so God took on our human identity and fixed it in the costliest way imaginable: God took on our sin.

This is where it matters that we know what it means to be human. To safeguard us from our own sin, God took it on. The cross of Jesus Christ, with all its cosmos-shattering implications in the very being of God who is complete in love and yet goes down to ignominious death is the place where our understanding fails, because we are not God. We do not know what that cost. We do not know what violence God took into God's self for us. We can't. We are limited in our understanding. But we can know that it is grace. It is love. It is God's unfailing reliability.

So, maybe we don't say "We're only human" anymore.

Maybe, let's say instead, "I want to do better."

Or maybe we could say instead, "I love you."

And perhaps we could think of grace and peace abounding, the way God wants it.

One of our members here likes to sign her e-mails, "Grace all over."

I love that. It's the heart of the Gospel: there's grace all over.

It reminds me of a favorite quote of mine, from Frederick Buechner,

"The grace of God means something like: Here is your life. You might never have been, but you *are* because the party wouldn't have been complete without you. Here is the world. Beautiful and terrible things will happen. Don't be afraid. I am with you. Nothing can ever separate us. It's for you I created the universe. I love you."[9]

A little lower than God, crowned with glory and honor, that's what it is to be human.

In the name of the Father, and of the Son, and of the Holy Ghost, Amen.

---

[9] Frederick Buechner. *Wishful Thinking: A Seeker's ABC.* (HarperOne: SanFrancisco, 1993 p 9

Part Two

Response: Exhortations to Action

The Kingdom and the Chasm
Luke 16:19-31

Churches are supposed to be places of grace and it is a deeply jarring experience when a congregation takes a hard turn away from grace toward judgmentalism. I had a conversation with a friend of mine recently about this very thing. My friend had drifted away from church. It's a very typical pattern, it often happens in college, during the years when staying up late on Saturday nights doesn't yet involve paying for it four days afterward. And she said she never really felt drawn back to church until the moment she realized her darling infant has become a screaming toddler who is careening down a scary path and it seemed like a good time to find some religion. Or at least some similarly challenged company. So she started attending a little church down the street from her home and joined. A few years later I was catching up with her again and asked her how her church was. She looked me dead in the eye and said, "I don't think I'll mess with that anymore. I mean, I'm trying to teach my children how to be kind and decent to people and every time I turned around, there was another sermon about who wasn't suitable in God's house. I think my children can just do without that."

My own family experienced something rather jarring in much the same way when the church in which my father grew up took a hard turn toward extreme pietism. Piety, or the living of faith practices to enrich faith is a good thing. But piety when it is lived for other reasons can veer off the path of faith onto the path of self-righteousness, and from there it is a slippery slope to judgmentalism. As my father grew more and more restless with what he was hearing and ultimately joined my mother's Presbyterian church, I was largely, happily oblivious. It wasn't until years later that I realized how profound the effect of drifting from grace to judgmentalism could be for someone in formative years. I realized it when my brother, who is ten years older than I am, said to me one day, "I heard enough about weeping and gnashing of teeth when I was a child to last me the rest of my life. If I ever hear the words come out of your mouth, 'verily, verily I say unto thee,' I'm headed for the door. I've had enough of that."

The church is about grace, and it is jarring when we encounter anything else.

And yet, the transition from the 15th chapter of Luke to the 16th gives virtual theological whiplash as the reader, flush with the grace of the finding of the lost sheep and lost coin and finally, the return of the prodigal – the finding of a lost son, full of grace, rushes headlong into the stony slab of the 16th chapter, full of love of money and rich men suffering in Hades. It is a harsh transition, seemingly a schizophrenic God vacillating between mercy and torment.

At a glance, this parable seems bereft of grace. This parable appears to contain judgment. And perhaps it does. But, the Gospel is about grace, and so we need to struggle with this text a bit more, without running from it, and consider what word it might in fact offer us.

We may be perfectly comfortable with this text. I, for one, don't think of myself as a rich man. I have absolutely no complaints, but this preacher just doesn't count himself as being among the rich. Indeed, as my friend Tom Long preached on this text a number of years ago, it can be deeply satisfying in reading this parable to see a rich man get what he has coming to him. It can be extremely gratifying in a world in which we see pampered stars and ballplayers behaving extremely badly using large sums of money to do so, or when our economy looks like an episode of "billionaires gone bad," to think to ourselves, "Yeah. This is right. This is just. The rich got it for a change." There's just one problem with this line of thinking. It doesn't really matter whether or not I count myself among the rich, according to the measures of the world, I am. And so are you.

There is a website called "the global rich list" and it takes a measurement of one's relative wealth against the rest of the world. You can do it by income or wealth. I chose income. It's simplistic to be sure and it doesn't factor cost of living or anything like that, but if subsistence can be measured by what takes to get by, surely wealth can be measured by what one has in excess of what it takes the least wealthy to get by. So, having been challenged by a minister friend of mine to see where I stood, I anted up and entered a figure roughly my annual salary into the little conversion machine. I was astonished, astonished to learn that I am approximately the 3.7 millionth richest person in the world. Sure, by their metric, approximately 3.7 million people in the world make more than I do. But over six billion have less. I'm in the top 6/00 of a percent. Just for fun, I tried wealth. I still couldn't break below the top five percent. I'm not richer or poorer than this congregation. No matter where we fall in the economic spectrum today, no matter what pressures we feel, compared with huge swathes of the globe, we have it pretty good. So, Tom said, "Whatever this parable has to say to the rich, it has to say to us."[10]

---

[10] Thomas Long. *A Great Chasm.* Gilchrist Sermon, preached at Trinity Presbyterian Church, Charlotte, NC.

So we can't take comfort in seeing the rich get their due. And as such, perhaps we need to think more about this parable.

Now, nowhere do I find in the pages of scripture a condemnation of the rich simply for being rich. Shockingly, as much as Jesus had to say about money, it was generally about what we do with it, not about the condition of having it. Money in the Gospel is pretty value neutral. It is what is done with it about which Jesus concerns himself.

Now what I think is pretty clearly not the case in this story based on its context is the blanket, eternal condemnation of folks based on economics. A facile glance at the parable might offer that assessment, but that would be wrong. First, paying attention to the context, it is clear that this chapter is sandwiched amidst stories of inclusion, mercy, kindness and forgiveness. In the stories of grace of chapter 15, no one, not even the rich, is left out. Second, there's a clue embedded in the text that I have often missed.

Tom once told me of an ancient practice of storytelling employed by the rabbis. They would periodically tell what were called, "Eleazar of Damascus" stories. They weren't necessarily Biblical, but they made their point. Who, you may ask, is Eleazar of Damascus? He is Abraham's heir in Genesis, before the covenant is fulfilled yielding offspring. A Biblical character hardly worth noting. But when the rabbis would tell the Eleazar stories, they were stories about Eleazar being sent to earth on an errand to point to the kingdom of God. The stories always featured Eleazar coming, incognito, disguised as a shepherd or a beggar, to point to the kingdom of God. So these rabbis would tell the stories of the kingdom of God being right in front someone, right there, so close it could be tasted, with Eleazar pointing the way, and do you know how Eleazar translates from Hebrew to Greek? Lazarus.[11]

Lazarus has something to say to us.

We in the church are not generally accustomed to hearing a voice of judgment. Hopefully we are not ourselves judgmental, but generally, I know we try to be good people, and by and large, I think we are, so the idea of a parable offering us judgment rather than grace is more than a little disconcerting, particularly when the language of the parable is strong language, perhaps scary language. But judgment isn't about punishment or imputing guilt. Judgment, in the Biblical tradition, is about making something right. In that sense, we must understand that God's judgment is full of grace. And certainly, if we look at the stories before and after this parable, we see

---

[11] Ibid.

stories full of grace. But right here in the middle we have this reminder… and it is a reminder of being watchful for the kingdom of God. And where is the kingdom of God? It is where generosity, kindness and mercy abound.

You see, what I think Luke wants us to avoid is cheap grace. We know cheap grace when we see it. It's grace that is misunderstood. When God gives us grace you see, it is to transform us, our situations, our relationships and our lives from a broken state where we don't live as though we were created in God's image, made for community, fellowship and love, to a redeemed state where, even when we miss the mark, we are still striving for the kingdom to which Eleazar is pointing, that place of generosity, kindness and mercy. Cheap grace is grace that has missed the point.

The rich man, suffering in torment, cries out to father Abraham, "Have mercy on me and send Lazarus down here to cool my throat." It's as if he's learned nothing.

"Child," says Abraham, "there is a great chasm between us."

"Well, then, send him to warn my brothers that they may avoid this torment."

I have struggled to determine just what that chasm is that cannot be bridged. I may be way out on a limb; I could be missing the mark, but I think perhaps the chasm that cannot be bridged is that of cheap grace. The rich man's concern remains himself. Failing to secure relief for himself, he tries to turn Lazarus into an errand boy to enable his brothers to avoid torment themselves. Nothing has changed.

Grace as a failsafe against perceived future torment is cheap because it misses the point. It's not grace; it's cosmic hell insurance. It misses the point.

There is a chasm of cheap grace fixed between just covering one's own eternity and looking for the kingdom of God.

"Child," says Abraham, "there is a chasm between us." That is not the language of judgmentalism, it is the language of lament. It is the lament that all around, God is offering grace and when it is turned into something other than what it is meant to be, there may as well be a canyon between where we are and the kingdom of God.

In grace, God is offering us judgment, a chance to see one of those glimpses of the kingdom, as a situation is made right, fixed, redeemed. In cheap grace, all we may find is judgmentalism.

You can't bridge the gap between cheap grace and the mercy of God. They are too different. They are too far apart.

There is a lot of cheap grace around. There always has been. Indeed, that has often been my critique of revivalist preaching. I sometimes come down hard on fundamentalist preachers, and I don't want to critique the sincerity of the preachers or the worshippers, but if the primary and only concern is saving one's skin, or one's soul, or avoiding future torment, I'm not sure that grace has really happened. And my question for us is whether our worship, but more, our lives, is full of grace for each other?

You see, I don't believe the point of this parable is that if you've been materially wealthy in this life you're going to suffer in the next. I don't believe that's Luke's point because it would be inconsistent with the message of the Gospel that grace transforms us. But maybe this parable is poised there for the Pharisees who are full of *phylargoria* – love of money… they were stunted with the love of money. And here's this story saying, "Look, look, there's the kingdom of God… come on in! Don't miss it."

These Pharisees are quoting scripture to justify themselves… they were looking back to the Hebrew Scriptures and there finding a deuteronomic proof-text to justify the idea that if they're wealthy, it means God is blessing them, and if someone is poor, well then, God must be punishing them and it is best not to interfere with the work of God. So, pardon me, while I step over you famished beggar and go to my abundance, because my prosperity is clearly God's doing. Now that sounds silly, but we can find that attitude today. I think it was called *The Prayer of Jabez* a few years ago, and I remember some green prosperity handkerchiefs being shilled a few years earlier on late night cable. There's a great chasm.

Parables are stories. They're wisdom shared in a way we might overhear the Gospel and not miss the kingdom.

But grace is not cheap, and the calling of the church is not to miss grace because we got caught up in something else.

Even with grace abounding, it's so easy to get caught up in something else… I've done it; you've done it. The kingdom was right there… right there and we were too busy with something else.

But the kingdom is all around us, and sometimes, sometimes we see it. Many years ago, I led a mission trip of the church I served at the time with my brother and one of our dearest friends. It was in an urban area, and we had taken the youth for ice cream. That's a staple of youth ministry, it's a bribe the advisors give to the youth for working hard and being good and being in an urban area, we were naturally near areas where significant poverty was evident, but also where the businesspeople during the day would come for lunch. As it happened, the ice-cream shop happened to be next to a Chinese restaurant and an abundance of impoverished people, probably without homes. Now in these urban immersion mission experiences, we are all repeatedly admonished not to give out cash. Buy a meal if you wish, donate to the agencies who are equipped to help, but DO NOT GIVE OUT CASH! Of course, we were asked for food right in front of the kids. Realizing that the hypocrisy of brushing past the homeless on a mission trip to get to the ice-cream parlor would send the wrong message to our youth, the two advisors decided to teach an object lesson. We huddled, and it was decided that I would take the youth for ice cream and they go into the restaurant and buy his dinner and take it to him since he wasn't allowed in. When about twenty minutes passed, I began to become concerned. After another twenty minutes, when the shop was closing, the other advisors appeared. Having spent 45 minutes herding the band of cats known as adolescent youth by myself, I wanted an explanation. Sheepishly, the two advisors said, well, we went in to buy him dinner and every time we came out with a meal, there was someone else waiting to ask us to help and you all were only forty feet away and invariably, one of the kids was watching. That object lesson just cost us just shy of two hundred dollars! It only ended because the restaurant closed. And you know, we laughed about it all the way back to the church. And it was only later, much later; that I realized that it was the kingdom of God.

Don't miss it. Don't miss it.

In the name of the Father and of the Son and of the Holy Ghost, Amen.

How Much Do You Owe?
Jeremiah 8:18-9:1; Luke 16:1-13

Well, let's see if we can't take the teeth out of this parable, shall we?

To be perfectly honest, I don't think any of us much like it, what with that talk about choosing between money and God.

What's more, despite the old admonition, "neither a borrower nor a lender be," I suspect a great many of us are both borrowers and lenders. We mortgage our homes. We invest our money in the stock market. We need a certain amount of money to navigate life. We are both borrowers and lenders.

And I suspect that is just the beginning of the ways that our lives are not the same as the lives of those listening to Jesus.

For instance, we don't live in a subsistence economy.

The closest I have ever truly come to a subsistence economy was when I was in Alaska a number of years ago. There I was leading a group who had gone to Alaska for a mission trip to a local Indian tribe. (I would say *Native American*, and they would correct me and say, "No, we're *Indians.*")

Our hosts brought us a beautiful fresh caught salmon, plucked right out of the water off the end of the pier, and I remarked that it was enough to feed an army – there was no way that our group could possibly eat it all. Could they keep a portion?

My host remarked that they would be risking their right to sell their fishing rights if they were caught with more than the subsistence quota in their freezers.

That's sort of different from the subsistence economy that Jesus would have known. That's not to say that there weren't wealthy people in Jesus' day, or that people didn't hoard money, I'm sure they did.

But we could fairly say that our methods and metrics surrounding business are certainly different from what Jesus would have encountered when he told this parable.

Lending is regulated. Borrowing is regulated. Investing is carefully controlled.

This story wouldn't happen now. Nobody would knowingly wipe out the debt of all of their clients today. And even if they wanted to, I'm sure there's something to prevent it. I am a theologian, not a banker, so I don't understand all the ins and outs of investment banks versus commercial banks, but I suspect a great number of you do, and I suspect you could elaborate for me all the ways that such an accounting fraud could be prevented.

In other words, there are a million ways not to see ourselves in this passage.

See how easy that was? There's the parable, but no harm is done to us in reading it. We don't have to adjust a thing about our lives. It applies to them, not us, we can avoid its deeper claims.

But a certain amount of honesty is called for in reading it, though, don't you think?

If we're honest, we know at a deep level that we all *do* owe something.

Perhaps you remember a little snippet I shared with you a while back about when Fred Rogers accepted a lifetime achievement award for his work on *Mister Rogers' Neighborhood?*

I shared the observation that, given the chance to harangue Hollywood for the drivel that led him to start filming *Mr. Rogers' Neighborhood*, Fred Rogers instead asked the gathered audience to remember someone who had loved them into being who they were in that moment, whether a parent, a teacher, whomever. The story goes that within fifteen seconds, in silence, the camera panned over the audience of celebrities and producers and stars, and observed that tears were beginning to run down the faces of the gathered people. Soon after, the sound of muffled sobs could be heard.

We all owe somebody something.

Indeed, Frank Bruni picked up on this back in 2012 in a column he wrote for the New York Times entitled, *Individualism in Overdrive.*[12]

Bruni notes in his column that in recent years the number of Americans drawing Social Security disability has tripled. He notes that to a certain extent it could be related to a liberalization of the requirements to apply and better understanding of what constitutes disability in the medical community. But

---

[12] *NYT*, July 16, 2012

then he notes that alone couldn't account for the increase. There are at least a few who are gaming the system. He writes,

"I've known a few of them. I bet you have, too. Making a mockery of all the Americans who rightly depend on such aid, they exaggerate impairments, pressing doctors to validate their conditions on the theory that no harm is really done, not when they're suckling at a teat as elastic and amorphous as the Federal Treasury."

But then he notes, "But that treasury is the sum of us – our deposits and withdrawals – and to cheat it is to cheat your neighbor. It's really that simple."[13]

Just as the treasury is the sum of all the depositors, every person, every human is the sum of all that has been expended to make them who they are. If I'm not mistaken, that is the heart of humanism, at least its renaissance form.

We all owe somebody something. To pretend otherwise is to be either an ingrate or delusional. Unless you managed to conceive, birth and raise yourself, you didn't raise yourself and you weren't raised by wolves. Even if you had horrible parents and a rotten childhood, even if you were failed over and over again, you are still part of a web of interconnectedness that is inescapable.

If you were educated at a school where someone else paid the teachers' salary, you owe somebody something.

Indeed, as I think of what it means to be *human*, increasingly I come to believe it is the reality of connection. As Paul says, "I cannot say I have no need of you." It's just factually wrong to think that any of us can claim to be entirely self-made.

We all owe somebody something – and living into the fullness of that is what makes a good life.

It's not earth shattering. In fact, I sort of like the way Fred Craddock puts it:

"The life of a disciple is one of faithful attention to the frequent and familiar tasks of each day, however small and insignificant they may seem...the realism of these sayings is simply that life consists of a series of seemingly small opportunities. Most of us will not this week Christen a ship, write a

---

[13] Ibid.

book, end a war, appoint a cabinet, dine with the queen, convert a nation or be burned at the stake. More likely the week will present no more than a chance to give a cup of water, write a note, visit a nursing home, vote for a county commissioner, teach a Sunday School class, share a meal, tell a child a story, go to choir practice and feed the neighbor's cat."[14]

I like that. There's a certain realism to it, isn't there? We recognize what we can do. We tend to our little corner of the universe and make it as good as it effectively can be. We do as much as we can for those whom we can and then we relax. It's like a lite version of John Wesley's old quote we're hearing these days, "Do all the good you can. By all the means you can. In all the ways you can. In all the places you can. At all the times you can. To all the people you can. As long as ever you can."

You know, don't worry about releasing the captives and proclaiming good news to the blind, just beautify your corner of the world.

And with that, we have effectively rendered our parable for today utterly and completely toothless. It won't harm anyone ever again like this. "We all owe somebody, we can't pay it back, we pay it forward as much as we feel like we owe, and nobody loses an eye."

We've rendered it utterly useless by sublimating it under a crushing weight of classical humanism.

Now mind you, I like Classical Humanism. I like it a lot. Calvin was a humanist, at least in the renaissance since. Erasmus was a humanist. We recognize our interconnectedness. We recognize what our interconnectedness does for common life together and thus act accordingly. We note what we owe to one another and society. We fence out individualism in overdrive and live our best lives now and we leave it at that. By this standard, Jesus himself is a humanist.

But Jesus got something that I think we want to forget. Jesus understood sin.

We don't like sin much, do we? Why should we? It's evil. Literally, it's evil. We avoid it. We don't want to talk about it. We don't want to confront it. So we joke. We back away from it. We don't want to sit and stare at what it has done to our lives.

---

[14] Fred Craddock. *Luke* in *Interpretation*. Westminster/John Knox Press: Louisville, 1990. P 192

We don't want to consider that if you had horrible parents and a rotten childhood that it is sin that is the root and cause of that.

We don't want to spend much time on the unpleasantness of a miserable marriage because that means looking at sin head on and naming it, and indeed, fighting it.

And the ugliest thing about sin is that when all things are equal, sin always wins. Violence begets more violence. Those who are abused are statistically trapped into becoming abusers themselves.

I could go on, you get it.

In the absence of disrupting forces, sin wins. Jesus knew that.

Even with disrupting forces, the deck is stacked against change. We want to revert to form.

I really don't mean to harp on sin, but if we're going to talk about it, we may as well at least be honest about it… sin makes that web of interconnectedness that God made to support us and love us into our full humanity into a twisted net that traps us in suffocating self-interest.

We always have to be honest, right? I mean, we promised these children that we'd be honest with them. We promised that we'd live a Christian life, and that by what we say and what we do, we'll show them that, right? You were telling the truth?

Because the parable is pretty harsh; not so much in the wiping away of debts and the fact that the manager gets away with it. It's harsh because Jesus says you can't serve God and money. He follows it up, right away, with another parable, this time of a rich man who ignores the poor in his lifetime and is left suffering the torments of hell afterwards. He's talking to Pharisees, and he's lecturing them on the sin of Phylargoria – that's the love of money – Luke doesn't think much of rich people, by the way, he sort of spits it out when he's dealing with rich people, and that's a problem for us because Luke would definitely include us in the rich – you and me both. I don't think of myself as a rich man, but according to Luke, I am and you are, and so we must pay attention to this story, and we must take it seriously. To do so, we always put it in the larger story.

Luke's pretty critical of wealth – he's critical of how we get it and why we're not doing more with it than we are to make the world better – but the Gospel doesn't begin and end with this parable and its shocking admonition.

The Gospel begins with the incarnation and it ends with the resurrection. It begins with God loving humankind enough to become human, and it ends with God loving humankind enough to go down to death for us and the vindication of that death is the resurrection. That's what we owe. We didn't make this world. We had it all and then we mucked it up. And what's more, we didn't redeem it, Jesus did.

We owe it all.

No, you really can't serve God and money. You have to choose.

Let me end with a story Tom Tewell shares of a man out west who lived his whole life on a family farm, a ranch, working the land, hunting for game, fishing for food, working hard his whole life. Then he struck oil. Soon the ranch was producing barrel after barrel of the stuff and the man was loaded. His children began to squabble over shares. One day he was talking to Tom and he said, "When I was younger, I worked the land. If we needed food, I hunted. I pulled fish from the pristine river and my children and I would feast. I didn't know it, but I was rich.

Now all I have is money."

No, you can't serve two masters. You will have to choose. But as far as what you owe –

That's been taken care of.

In the name of the Father, and of the Son, and of the Holy Ghost, Amen.

Jail Break
Luke 4:16-30

My friend Andy Odom tells the story of a man he knew of years ago who was something of a barfly and self-styled evangelist.

He would sit at the bar and make small talk with whomever he met, and if all remained relatively kind-spirited he would simply blend into the crowd, watch a ball game or whatever was on television and just be one of the guys.

But, if the conversation turned mean our hero would perk up and listen. If it involved gender roles or sexuality or anything that had even a whiff of Biblical literalism, he would sidle into the conversation, listening for the Bible to be used to demean or marginalize someone, and as the conversation progressed, he would lie in ambush, waiting for the inevitable appeal to the authority of the Scripture to solidify whatever claim was being made.

Then he would pounce. He would insert himself into the conversation with the words, "I've been looking for some Bible-believing Christians. Are you all Bible-believing Christians?"

Having been suckered in through his earnestly sincere demeanor, the unsuspecting adherent to questionable Biblical authority would generally respond by taking the bait.

"Yes I am."

Just to be sure, our hero would then set the hook: "I have been looking for Bible-believing Christians – now you're sure you're Bible-believing Christians?"

As soon as person across the bar affirmed his or her status as a Bible-believing Christian, our hero would spring the trap:

"Great! I've some sledgehammers in the truck, let's go over to the county jail and release us some captives!"

This is when the hapless victim would generally begin backing away.

Our hero would press the question: "You said you believed in the Bible? Well doesn't the Bible proclaim release for the captives?"

Well, what about it? What *does* the Bible say about release for captives? Or sight for the blind? How about freedom for the oppressed?

For the Biblical literalist, I suppose the answers are at least clear if perhaps a bit distasteful where the release of prisoners might be concerned, or the freedom for the oppressed. The directive one would follow would be easy enough to understand because understood Biblically, both concepts would hearken back to the ancient Israelite practice of jubilee, where every so often, slaves were freed, and land was returned to its original owners – it was a sort of way of assuring that nobody was ever permanently on the outside. It was a way of assuring, not necessarily that poverty was eliminated, but that slavery and debt slavery were not a permanent part of the way of life of God's people. Though it was commanded by God in Leviticus, there are no records that indicate it happened. But it was important enough to their identity that it made it into the Law.

Now, for those of us who take guidance from the prophet Nehemiah, who instructs us to seek interpretation of scripture using its own pages as our guide, well, I'm not sure it is particularly easier.

Jesus' sermon in his home synagogue was something else.

I was invited back to preach at my home church a couple of times. The last time was at least ten years ago. I'm not sure what I said.

Luke says they were ready to throw him off a cliff.

I guess I got off easy.

Luke uses this story a little differently from Matthew and Mark. They place this story later in their telling of the Gospel. For them, it's just a tale about a sermon gone wrong; every preacher has one. Jesus merely offends, the people have no faith and only a handful of folks get healed.

For Matthew and Mark, nobody is hurling anyone off a cliff.

Luke raises the stakes. This story is early in his telling of the Gospel narrative, and it is a story designed to offend because it is a *prophetic* story.

It is a prophetic story because it suggests to its hearers that there is a way that God wants to see people go, and it is not the way that the hearers are going.

Luke puts this story early, right on the heels of Jesus' baptism and temptation narratives because he wants to set a tone right from the start: the nature of Jesus' teaching and ministry is to be *prophetic*.

It is not the prophetic preaching necessarily that offends Jesus' hometown. It is rather the radical scope that his sermon suggests for God's grace that sends them, as it were, over the edge. Anyone paying close attention would have heard Simeon's pronouncement in the temple and the citation of Isaiah earlier as hallmarks that Jesus ministry is going to be radically inclusive, with salvation extending to all the nations, which is just a way of saying all the people.

New Testament scholar Luke Timothy Johnson puts it this way:

"It is this veiled intimation that the prophet would be for all and not just for them – and in the reader's understanding, that God's visitation and salvation were to be for the poor and oppressed of all nations and not just for Jews – that arouses the neighbors' wrath, impelling them to fulfill Jesus' statement: he is not acceptable in his own country because his ministry extends beyond that of his own country. Luke thus provides the last part of the prophetic pattern, that of rejection by the people."[15]

For those of you paying attention here, it is no doubt clear what is going on: Jesus has quit preaching and gone to meddling.

Prophecy offends because prophecy dares to state that how it is now is not how it always will be, and for those who are comfortable now, how it will be is not necessarily going to be comfortable or easy.

Make no mistake about my prophetic tendencies today. If I fall anywhere in this story, it is with those who would hurl Jesus off a cliff because his sermon chides my status as a relatively wealthy, relatively safe and relatively comfortable person. That I suspect, is the status of most of us gathered here.

Prophetic preaching is not easy to hear for those of us from whom the prophecy demands action.

I have never been a Biblical literalist, so I don't fully understand the grip of that sin. But literalism is sin because it is idolatry – literalism sets our fixed notion of the words above God's living Word.

---

[15] Luke Timothy Johnson. *Luke*. (The Liturgical Press: Collegeville, MN, 1991) p 82

But for most of us, the meaning of this passage doesn't involve hitching the pickup to a prison wall to engineer a jail break. Nor am I under the illusion that glasses are no longer going to be necessary for those who can't see, and as one walking around with a substantial hearing loss, I understand the coming of Jesus hasn't removed my need for a hearing aid. But we miss the point if we dwell on the infirmities.

When Jesus cites Isaiah and claims the scripture is fulfilled, the whole world is turned upside down. The outsiders were going to be let in, the infirm are going to be made whole.

That's what offended! That's what had that congregation ready to throw him off a cliff… Jesus messed with their sense of being special and set aside because he just said all these marginalized people are going to take over the church.

Prophecy tends to offend.

If God is going to *claim* all of these unwell, unwhole, unclean people… well, what does that leave us?

For some of us, it means we have to give up the category of outsider – clinging to our separation can be as addictive as leaving people out.

For all of us, it means that forgiveness extends further than just the folks we like.

It means we have this extraordinary calling to be more than we think we can.

Of course, that way of life is often caricatured as idealistic and unrealistic, and Christianity has always found to ways to deal with the idealistic and unrealistic.

Douglas John Hall describes both in his book, <u>The Steward, a Biblical Symbol Come of Age</u>.

Here is how Hall suggests we have managed the enormity of the calling of Jesus' sermon in Nazareth: one way is to exercise what he calls theocentrism and the other is to rely upon Christian humanism.

Now these are grossly simplified but here is what he means:

With *theocentrism*, we can push it all off to the sweet by and by. The function of the church is to point the world to God and as long as we are doing so, we can trust that folks will do what they need to and even if they don't, as long as we are winning converts to Jesus, we're doing what the Lord requires. All will be made well in the kingdom, which is at some point yet-to-be determined. Winning souls for Jesus is the point, not alleviating suffering in the here and now, because clearly, the poor will be with us always. Maybe you've heard this one?

Option two, *Christian humanism*, is a bit more sympathetic to the poor, but has little hope for resolving the present problems of the world. Sure, they're insurmountable, but that shouldn't stop us from throwing everything we have at sharing the plight of the poor and oppressed. Where *theocentrism* can be caricatured as winning souls for Jesus, Christian humanism can be accused of throwing money, food, etc at a problem idealistically hoping to make it go away. I'm sure you've seen this too.

Neither approach can contain the Gospel.

The point of the Gospel according to Hall, requires us to understand that the one calling us to win souls or feed the hungry is the one who preached his way on to a cross for our sakes.

The end of the sermon wasn't the cliff in Nazareth, it was the cross in Jerusalem.

And so, it is that any prophetic message we may hear must share in terms of a costly grace.

It is as easy to declare that everyone is welcome and that God has broken down the dividing walls of hostility and made us ministers of reconciliation if all we must do is win souls for Jesus or give money.

But putting our whole selves on the line is another matter.

That means that forgiveness and grace can't be cheap. And so, it requires breaking down the barriers of captivity within *ourselves*, recovering *our* sight, leaping to dance with joy in spite of *our* lameness, and believing we have been freed from the oppression of *our* own sin and pain. *The Jail-Break is for us!!!*

The prophetic word requires the hearer to give up something… to give up old grudges… or old prejudice… or old hurt. The prophetic word is not easy to hear because it means *we will be changed*.

67

A little less than twenty years ago, I walked around a cemetery in Scotland where the victims of the bombing of Pan Am 103 are buried. Their families placed stones remembering them.

A while back, you may recall, the terminally-ill Pan Am 103 bomber was released on compassionate grounds by the Scottish government in order that he could go home to die.

He returned home to a hero's welcome.

I was offended. Many Americans were offended.

When I e-mailed back and forth with Marion and John, the wonderful couple in Scotland who offered me enormous hospitality during my exchange, Marion expressed her surprise that we Americans didn't understand that it was the value of compassion that motivated the Scots' action.

"No," I replied, "It was the hero's welcome that offended us."

"Well," Marion said, "does that diminish the need for compassion on our parts?"

"The Spirit of the Lord is upon me," said Jesus, "because he has anointed me to bring good news to the poor. He has sent me to proclaim *release* to the captives and recovery of sight to the blind and to let the oppressed go free to proclaim the year of the Lord's favor."

Are there any Bible-believing Christians in here?

In the name of the Father and of the Son, and of the Holy Ghost, Amen.

A Primer on Defiling Oneself
Mark 7:1-8, 14-23

Perhaps you've heard the old adage, "Bad decisions make the best stories."

My older brother is an emergency physician in North Carolina. He could and would readily give the anecdotal support for that adage… frequently his best stories involve the campers at the infield at the Coca Cola 600. It's not pretty.

One year, for Christmas, I gave him a copy of *Darwin Awards*. Are you familiar with *The Darwin Awards?* It's really quite a horrible book – it's folks who remove themselves from the gene-pool in particularly spectacular fashion. The case studies aren't funny, but the near misses can be a good read… One good example is of an environmentalist who wanted to make a point of conservation by depriving people of electricity. He contrived to do so by sawing through a 69,000-volt line. With a tree saw. Wearing dishwashing gloves for insulation.

Apparently with excellent medical care, he has suffered no permanent damage.[16]

Anyhow, I gave Brent this book one year, and he said, "I don't need to read this. My job is fighting natural selection *every single day.*"

Of course, the point is that foolishness is really only funny when nobody loses an eye.

The same is true of what *defiles* a person.

If you think the topic of defiling oneself is a cheery topic for a Sunday morning, I can assure you it was no cheerier when I sat down to write this past week. It's particularly lovely when we anticipate a baptism.

I don't know that we often give much thought to defilement as a matter of weekly course.

I know I periodically joke about the fine establishments that one encounters periodically along Cheshire Bridge road, but it's just jokes because there's really nothing funny about what goes on in the less savory places.

---

[16] http://darwinawards.com/stupid/stupid2008-04.html

Well, maybe that one sign, you know that one that claims that a particular bar is just like Cheers? That one has always struck me funny because I'm pretty sure that what's going on in there suggests that, in fact, sometimes you *don't* "wanna go where everybody knows your name."

But you and I both know the truth is there is really nothing funny about being defiled.

This morning, we encountered two different perspectives on defiling oneself in Mark's Gospel.

First, we have the Pharisees assessing the behavior of the disciples.

Then we have Jesus' rebuttal of their point of view.

First, we have a human construct – a social pressure to observe the niceties of ritual hand washing.

Mind you, I have nothing against hand washing. Indeed, I am a great fan of it. But that is not what is going on here with the Pharisees. What we get from the Pharisees in this moment is a "gotcha game" with the law. This is using an arbitrary metric to determine what constitutes acceptable behavior.

Then we have Jesus' rebuttal. It's a particularly interesting rebuttal because Mark, who rarely interprets the story for the reader, tells us that Jesus is declaring all foods clean. It's a clarifying moment. It is Jesus saying to his disciples and to the Pharisees all at the same time, "Get your eye on the ball."

And then he outlines what defiles a person.

If you ever needed a primer on defiling yourself, here it is. It's a semi-systematic listing of paradigmatic things that one can do to defile oneself. It's semi-systematic, but not exhaustive. There are plenty more things one can do to defile oneself. And here's what strikes me about it – everything on it is a way to devalue and denigrate yourself or someone else.

Everything on this list is an opportunity to be *less than God created you to be*.

You know, nobody ever sets out to do that. It seems to sneak up, doesn't it?

It starts with an insecurity; a hang-up.

It slips into a need for affirmation.

Temptation sidles up, looking like an opportunity.

It slides into decision.

It slinks into action.

Jesus uses fornication and adultery as two great examples of defiling oneself.

I suspect it is because he knows how destructive to self and others these particular behaviors are. They are community destroyers because you can't do them by yourself. And they are humanity destroyers because they make us *less than we're created to be.*

In fifteen years of parish ministry, I have never once heard someone say in their pre-marital counseling that they wanted to be unfaithful to their spouse.

And yet if you didn't know there is a website dedicated to facilitating that before last week, you probably do now.

And the truth is, I'm not really interested in psychoanalyzing the architecture of an affair. Nor am I particularly interested in classifying persons as defiled or not.

We are interested in understanding redemption.

The Pharisees wanted to make faithfulness a practice of hand washing – and the like, whatever little rituals people come up with to dictate what makes a person a good person or a bad person.

Jesus wanted them to go much deeper, to take a hard look at what diminishes our humanity.

He targeted a few behaviors as representative.

Please note closely this: Jesus said nothing about what makes a person *good* or *bad*, he talked about what makes us less than we are created to be.

Behaviors can lift us up. And behaviors can tear us down. What we do makes a difference.

But behaviors can never define our ultimate worth.

Okay, so true confession. This past week, I was walking out the door of the welcome center and I'd been kvetching with Drew about particular mutual acquaintance we share and a most recent negative interaction and I said somewhat jokingly, "Can't we just acknowledge that he's a bad person and have done with it?"

Drew paused just long enough to force the better angels of my nature to make me to finish the sentence, "Yes, I get it, I know he's a beloved child of God, but Drew, he *is* a seriously trifling beloved child of God."

This is what I get for having a career where I'm surrounded by ministers.

You can defile yourself but you can never make yourself anything other than a beloved child of God.

Jesus really does want us to go deeper in our own faith than hand washing. He wants us to understand our own behavior and feelings. He wants us to understand what diminishes the humanity of ourselves and others.

It's really easy to talk a lot about *humanity* and *defilement* and to leave it way up in the air, esoteric really, as to what makes for goodness and faithfulness. I think that is why Jesus is so concrete in his answer to the disciples.

And I think that is why, from time to time, we need to be concrete also. We're going to pledge again in a few moments, that *by the manner of our lives* we will show another child of God what it means to be a follower of Jesus Christ.

That means asking concrete questions. If you want to know how to live a life that shows people that you're a follower of Jesus, *behavior matters.*

Here are a couple of sample questions:

Is it kind? - Is it helpful? -Is it necessary? -Am I going to regret this? -What might I be about to damage or destroy?

Here is a bigger question, *When I am sitting on the porch at "the Home" and I'm ninety years old, and I look back over my life, what will I wish I'd done right now?*

It would be very easy to turn this passage today into an object lesson, "Do this, don't do that."

As object lessons go, it's a pretty useful one – behavior should have limits. But if all we do today is consider the reasonable limits of human behavior for the reduction of suffering, we can answer that with Aristotle's *Ethics*.

But Jesus wants us to go deeper. This is not just about non-sensical non-choices, "Should I be nice, or should I be a jerk"

"Do I really want destroy this person's sense of feeling valued, or do I just want to get lucky?"

It's about something deeper. It's about developing an *internal* life, an honesty with self about who God created you to be, and then being that person.

God created you to *be* human, not to be defiled.

The problem with defiling oneself is that it erodes at the underpinning of humanity that is our birthright. It erodes at what God created us for.

God didn't make us for cheapness… no, this is the God who, "*from our mother's arms has blessed us on our way with countless gifts of love.*"

And just as a behavior can leave us feeling a little less human than we know we are, just as a bad decision can leave us feeling a little less integrated with ourselves and each other, so can a kindness begin the restorative work of redemption.

I read a wonderful essay last week by Brett Martin about a lunch he had with Jacques Pepin.

Martin had endured an excruciatingly slow-motion breakup that he said, "Left me living in the windowless basement of an old friend's house in Brooklyn. Mornings, I lay in the complete darkness, listening to the shuffling and creaking as he and his wife and two children prepared for the day. There had been a time when I still felt close to that domestic future, but now the truth of my life had been revealed: I was no man. I was a troll in the cellar. Of all the fallout, physical, psychological, and emotional – one effect was most worrisome: I had lost my appetite."

Broke, he took on a freelance assignment from a friend at GQ magazine, to interview one of the first celebrity chefs, Jacques Pepin, for his tips on designing a home kitchen.

He began the interview by apologizing for taking up the chef's time. "No, no, don't be ridiculous." Back and forth they went… gas stove, but electric oven… Freezer drawer, not side by side… Most gadgets are useless… As he prepared to leave, Pepin's assistant asked if he wanted something to eat. Assuming it was just a courtesy, he returned the courtesy asking, "Will you join me?"

Pepin, he wrote, "Looked at me as though I might have hearing problems. 'Of course! It's lunchtime.'"

As they ate, the chef asked, "What do you think of the consommé?"

It needed salt. But more than that, being treated like someone who should be asked was balm for his weariness. And so, as lunch progressed, Martin noted he realized his appetite was returning and he was ravenous. He grabbed hunks of bread and slathered them with paté. He gnawed the bones of the lamb chops. "If Pepin noticed, he didn't say."[17]

Amazing what lunch can do, no? No, not just any lunch – only one seasoned with human kindness.

This is what we are made for: human kindness… defilement is anything that violates that God-created reality.

Beloved child of God, I hope you'll wash your hands when they need to be washed, but so much more I hope you'll remember always that it is God who made you, and it is for *humanity* that you were made.

In the name of the Father, and of the Son, and of the Holy Ghost, Amen.

---

[17] Brett Martin. *The Chef Who Saved Me* in *The Week*. August 21, 2015. p 36

Like an Everflowing Stream
Amos 5:28-24, Matthew 28:1-13

Every once in a while, a text comes along that perplexes rather than answers questions. Amos by himself is one of my favorite proof-texts of scripture. The rhetorician in me just loves the parallelism of water rolling down and ever-flowing streams. But Amos with the bridesmaids in Matthew's Gospel leaves me afflicted with questions. And I see no reason that I should endure this state alone, so welcome to my world.

Now, Amos had a clear sense of what he was saying, and I expect its meaning is clear enough for us as well, but I wanted to know what others thought of these words, justice and righteousness, so I crowd-sourced the question, *What is Justice*, to social media last week to hear what folks have to say. If we're going to talk about justice rolling down like waters, it's probably good to know what we're talking about.

My favorite answer, by far, was the first one: a brand of cheaply made yet inexplicably expensive (insert adjective here) clothing for female tweens.

I'm not sure exactly what the tie in to clothing branding is, but it's not justice, and it's important to know the difference.

You know why it's important to know the difference and to live it?

It's because of that parade of children we saw last Sunday. If you weren't here, it was glorious. The doors opened, the choir sang, and scores of children walked down the aisle and lined the front of the sanctuary.

I was in my clergy group on Thursday and I heard a staggering statistic that 70% of children raised in mainline churches leave the church as adults – and of the 30% who do continue in faith as adults – the single factor that seemed to make a difference was whether or not the children saw faith modeled in their parents. 82% of those who were in church as adults said it was because they saw faith in their parents' lives. Not the quality of the programming, not whether the children considered church fun, not the status of the facility, solely whether or not the children saw discipleship in Jesus Christ being modeled by their parents.

That's why I send you letters in *The Messenger* saying that attending church is important. That's why giving is important. That's why prayer is important.

Sure, my ego loves a full sanctuary – every preacher likes an audience and an amen pew – but truthfully, it's because my calling, the whole church staff's calling, indeed, the whole church's calling is to help people be disciples of Jesus Christ, and I don't believe that can be sustained apart from Christian community. If we want the children of God of every age to have a life-sustaining faith, it's not achieved apart from Christian community – *that* sustains what is done in the home. Because make no mistake about it: practices, such as prayer, giving, worshipping and learning are the building blocks that the holy spirit uses to make disciples of Jesus.

I know this congregation loves our children – I love our children – and I'm unwilling to throw in the towel on 70% of them walking away from the church.

So, the calling before us is to live the faith. It's that simple. *We* have to live the faith. We have to be disciples of Jesus – and that means *tangible and commensurate actions*.

Which brings me back to the question of justice.

So, a handful of folks equated it with the legal code and getting what you deserve, but my favorite response of those was the one who went on to say, "Thank God that God doesn't give us justice, but rather mercy."

Indeed. Who among us really wants what we deserve?

Some folks quoted theologians – that's sometimes helpful. One quote from Walter Brueggemann was that justice means figuring out what belongs to whom and returning it to them.

That one's certainly politically challenging – I'll leave it alone for the moment, but if it troubles you, then we probably ought to think about why it's so problematic.

Another quoted Cornel West: Justice is what Love looks like in public.

I think there's merit to that one too – love in the abstract is really pretty useless. To be love, it needs tangible and commensurate expression.

"Love in action," was another definition from a friend in an inner-city congregation. "Identifying oppression and working to end it," was the response of a friend of mine who works with migrant workers.

Fundamentally, the question that each of us faces is whether we are on the side of justice or not, and if not, why, and if so, what is justice?

Here's what one Old Testament theologian writes, "The picture that the word 'justice' brings to mind in our western tradition is that of a woman, blindfolded, holding a set of balances before her. Thus 'justice' is a static concept, a noun, describing the achievement of fairness and equality and symbolized by the state of balance wherein all is at rest. The image Amos calls to mind is entirely different. Justice is like a surging, churning, cleansing stream. All is in motion and commotion. Nothing is at rest. The same language is used in Judges 5:21 to describe the 'torrent' of the Kishon River. This is the prophetic picture of justice, it is more like an onrushing torrent than a balanced scale."[18]

The answers I got from my crowd-source question went on, the one that spoke the most deeply to me were two pictures that showed three children standing to see a ball game over a fence. The first picture, labeled, *equality*, showed three equal height boxes with different height children trying to look over the fence. The tallest had a great view of the ballgame, the second could just see over the fence, but could see, and the third, a little boy, was standing on his box looking at the fence. The second picture had the same children, and each could see over the fence. The tall child stood on the ground and he could see over the fence. The middle child stood on a box, and he could see over the fence. The little boy had the tall child's box stacked on his own, and he, too, could see over the fence.

That last one is what Biblical justice looks like.

Does that image of justice work for you? If not, why? If so, what are you doing that is *tangible and commensurate*?

John Dominic Crossan, in his wonderful but challenging book on the Lord's prayer, pictures creation as a macrocosm of what we encounter in our own homes, with God as the divine head of household. His suggestion is that what we could consider good in our own households, if it were applied to us, represents what is good in creation. He writes, "What horrifies the Biblical

---

[18] James Limburg. *Hosea-Micah* in *Interpretation*. (John Knox Press: Louisville, 1988) p 107

conscience… is the *inequality* that destroys the integrity of the household and therefore dishonors the householder,"[19] by which, he means, God.

He asks the troubling questions, "In what sort of household are some members exploited by others? In what sort of household do some members have far less than they want and others far more than they need? What sort of Householder is in charge of such a house?"[20]

Maybe that question doesn't bother you.

But I doubt it. I expect it bothers most all of you deeply when you think about it and I expect it also perplexes you, just as it does me, as to what represents a workable response.

Or perhaps the question is, what represents a tangible and commensurate response?

Because I have to tell you something. There really isn't a question as to what represents Biblical justice. It's pretty clear.

What *is* a question is, "How do we live into it?"

I told Drew over lunch this week that this text didn't really bother me when I was an associate working with mission and youth, because I could tell you exactly how we were living into it. But now that I'm in the senior role and one of my primary responsibilities is worship, that first part of the scripture really gets under my skin, the part where God says, "I hate, I despise your festivals, and I take no delight in your solemn assemblies. Even though you offer me your burnt offerings and grain offerings, I will not accept them; and the offerings of well-being of your fatted animals I will not look upon. Take away from me the noise of your songs; I will not listen to the melody of your harps."

I mean, seriously, we love festivals. Who doesn't love a parade, right? My job is solemn ceremonies!

It would be easy to take this the wrong way, and if we take it as God despising our worship, I'm afraid we'll have missed the point. God does love it when we worship. God, after all, is the object of our worship. We don't come to

---

[19] John Dominic Crossan. *The Greatest Prayer: Rediscovering the Revolutionary Message of the Lord's Prayer.* (HarperOne: San Francisco, 2010) p 45
[20] Ibid.

get our tanks filled and feel good, we come because God has already filled us to overflowing and we need to respond.

What Amos is saying is that worship without discipleship is meaningless.

Worship is not limited to 11-12 on Sunday mornings sitting in a pew. Worship is all of life. We worship God with our discipleship as well. The one is inseparable from the other.

And if 70% of children raised in mainline churches walk away from the church that raised them, then we have a crisis on our hands. That's an epidemic.

Thank God the answer lies right in front of us: be disciples in all our lives and trust God with the rest of it. Live discipleship: every difficult, wonderful, gritty Godly bit of it, because God has already filled us to overflowing and told us what is good.

The parable we encountered from Jesus today might just look like it tells us to do the opposite – to hold onto and attempt to preserve what we do have in order to avoid being found wanting. Isn't that always the temptation? And doesn't life funnel us in that direction? Nobody wants to be the foolish bridesmaid, after all. But there's more going on. It's not just about the oil, it's about when bridegroom arrived – late. Sometimes, the kingdom takes an awfully long time to manifest itself. So, to have that extra flask of oil is to be prepared that sometimes it takes a long time to see the kingdom, and we need our flasks refilled.

And that, I think, has something to say to justice.

If we are going to be serious about justice, we have to be prepared to be disciples for a long time. We have to take a long view. We can't just think about now, we have to look way off into an uncertain future and know that what we're doing presently may or may not be what it takes to get into the place of the kingdom of God's justice.

You see, discipleship doesn't guarantee instant gratification. In fact, it just about guarantees the opposite. To be faithful disciples is to live a long obedience in the same direction, to live in the direction of justice.

Now the second clause of this marvelous turn of phrase involves righteousness. Let justice roll-down like waters, righteousness like an everflowing stream.

When Jesus talks about righteousness, do you know what he means?

He doesn't mean self-righteousness. Not ever. Jesus has a real problem with self-righteous people.

He means doing the right thing.

That's what we're called to do as disciples. The right thing.

So, last reference to my crowd-sourcing: I had a follow up conversation with the first respondent, the one with pithy opinions about the oddly named clothing line. She was swinging through the church office right as I was about to start writing, and I teased about her response, because in the great irony of things, she's a lawyer by training. And she replied, "The thing about justice is you know it when you see it."

I think more often than not, that's the truth.

I've been talking for a while now about justice, and a little bit about righteousness, and I suppose I ought to wrap it up – and you know I love to end with a story that wraps it all up and brings it home.

You know I love to tell you a story.

But here will be no closing story, because you are the stories. Tag, you're it. Your lives as Jesus' disciples tell a more compelling story than I ever could. So go. Go be justice-seeking, righteousness-doing disciples of Jesus. Live the faith, and your stories, like an everflowing stream, will fill all of our flasks.

In the name of the Father, and of the Son, and of the Holy Ghost, Amen.

Lost, Found and Sometimes, In the Way…
Luke 15:1-10

Some years ago, I had the occasion to return to the parish I served in Scotland during a pulpit exchange. Knowing I would be in in the area, I called my friend Elinor, with whom I had exchanged, and asked if it would suit for me to come to worship. She graciously replied that, most certainly it would, but that I should be advised that the worship service would be quite a bit different that day. She went on to write that her church, the Kildrum Parish, had opened its doors to a group called Causeway Prospects. This group is a Christian organization concerned with, in their own words, "working together with individuals with learning disabilities to insure they can lead fulfilled lives." Elinor wrote me that the clients of the Causeway Prospects would themselves be leading worship that day and so I should expect skits about Biblical stories.

So, on Sunday morning, I walked over to the church where Elinor warmly welcomed me and then she turned the service over the men and women served by Causeway Prospects and their advocates.

The texts they were to act out are our texts today, the parable of the lost sheep and the parable of the lost coin. As their advocates and teachers shepherded these adults gently in to the chancel, some wore their conditions visibly, such as those with Down Syndrome, some looked impoverished and some looked quite wealthy.

One woman stood off to the side, probably about 55 years old, beautifully dressed and impeccably coiffed – I assumed she was a leader until she stood awkwardly when she didn't understand the instructions until her friend came and took her by the hand and led her to where the others had moved. As we all watched, they read the stories about lost and found sheep and coins and acted them without self-consciousness.

I have to tell you about an insight that I am embarrassed to admit hit me like a thunderbolt.

As I was watching it quickly became evident to me that there were a variety of degrees of economic viability represented. As I sat in the pew and my mind wandered, I began to think of the reality that, if one is normally able, then economic hardship in life is an obstacle that we are taught, almost from birth in America, one can overcome. In our land of opportunity, and really in any land of opportunity, if you work hard, you'll probably do pretty well for yourself if economics are any measure. But if your abilities lie elsewhere and your brain processes information more slowly or in different ways, well, the evidence was clear: your station in life is your station in life and the advantages and disadvantages of class became all the more evident. As I sat in the pew, thinking of lost and found and who will seek the lost sheep, it struck me as a profoundly unfair thing that for those without advocates, the best you can get is the best the system offers, regardless of whether the system works or not. But that's not the thunderbolt. As I sat thinking of this reality – my mind grazed on over to thinking about the kingdom of God. As I sat there, I thought to myself, "Well, no doubt this is all true. But in the kingdom all is going to be made right. We will, doctrine teaches us, be made whole." I'm not being pietistic and I'm not trying to throw the tough ones off into the kingdom – that really was my thought process and for a brief second I found it comforting.

But here's where my musings got interesting to me. I thought of my dear friends' child who has Down Syndrome, and I thought, "well, what does whole look like for her? How does this get made right without fundamentally changing who she is?"

And that is when the thunderbolt hit me: "Who said she's the one who needs to be changed for this to be made right?"

Suddenly, I had a different perspective on who was lost.

Theologically *wholeness* is about the restoration of shalom, or God's reign of peace and justice. I know all that... but it was just so easy to slip into thinking of the categories of "lostness" and "foundness" based not on a vision of the kingdom but on what would be the easiest. It was much tougher to think of what *wholeness* would demand of me and you.

These parables are stories about great joy because that is grace at its very heart, and it is very tempting to locate ourselves in the parables – I think its unavoidable, really. We are people who relate to ourselves and others through stories and so when we encounter a parable, it's really tempting to assign parts as it were. And in the case of these parables in particular, it's even easier because two of the parts belong to an animal and an inanimate object. Three parts to be assigned in two stories: the Pharisee (they're the audience) and the lost and the seeker.

In a facile glance, the part of finder goes to Jesus. The part of coin/sheep goes to the sinners, and the part of the Pharisees will be played today by...

Now that's an easy glance and consequently, the lost are the sinners, the found are the saints and the Pharisees, well, we can either lump them in with the sinners or else just assume they are in the way.

That's an easy interpretation, but if that is the way we interpret it, these are parables dripping with judgmentalism, and that's not grace and it certainly isn't joy.

So, let's try again with these parables. Maybe we're the lost. Or maybe we're the found. Sometimes we might be the seeker (or at least the one working for the seeker) and sometimes, we're the sought. And grace being grace and not our doing, every once in a while, we're just in the way and God is up to something we haven't figured out yet.

I wonder sometimes if we don't rather enjoy being lost? If we are lost, then we're not responsible for our lack of direction. We're lost, Jesus is going to find us, and when he does, we'll have the great joy of being found. There's a whole thread of revivalist preaching that riffs along this theme: you're miserable sinners but Jesus loves you and if you accept him into your heart (again) you can be found!

I really don't mean to mock this line of thinking, but let's look at it critically. First, it makes being found an action of the lost – and second, it treats the condition of *lostness* trivially. Being lost – being fundamentally disoriented, unable to see the right way out, unable to retrieve oneself from the condition – that's not something to be considered trivially. Lostness is when the conditions required to pull oneself out are more than one could ever reasonably expect or be expected to manage alone. Addiction – lostness. Homelessness – lostness. Loneliness – lostness. Being lost is real. And any rescue from being lost is grace. And anything less than that is trivial.

We trivialize lostness and the accompanying grace when we act like sinners are the source of their own problems. To be sure, self-destructive behavior abounds and we bear responsibility for out bad actions, but grace – being found – isn't about saving ourselves, grace is about the transformative inbreaking of kindness.

Before we move on to the concept of "foundness" I do want to touch once more on that idea that we're all lost – because we are. Sin is, at its heart, the rejection and breaking of Shalom, or God's peaceable, just vision for the world. We all participate in it, whether we want to or not. So, sin isn't just lying, cheating, stealing and committing adultery, though those activities certainly qualify – sin is primarily participation in a system that is fundamentally unjust and unpeaceful – broken. If we are honest about God's vision for creation, we know that as long as violence and poverty persist, this isn't it. So we are all lost, in need of being found. That's why Reinhold Niebuhr reminded us that we sin in our best deeds as well as our worst. That is why sitting in that Scottish Church, I had the profound realization that I had, in fact, missed the point.

Now we can think about being found. If being lost is the condition of being trapped in a dystopia, then being found must surely be the participation in a utopia.

Well, not so realistically. The kingdom hasn't come. There is plenty of evidence to remind us that is not the case. But being found doesn't mean being perfect yet. Being found means working for the kingdom and being an agent of grace.

You know what grace is – I like this working definition: grace is the unmerited, undeserved, unconditional love of God. Nothing we do causes it, nothing we do can escape it… God decided to love us and to do so unconditionally. It's why we are simultaneously lost and found, both sinner and saint. That's why foundness is not something to brag about, it's something profoundly to celebrate and share. Grace is not a commodity to be proud of but a gift to share. Which is why we, being both lost and found can ultimately be the seeker, on behalf of the one who sought us, because grace is not about what we've done, grace is always about what God is doing. That is the grace we celebrate in baptism – that God is doing something, sometimes despite our efforts! That's why we baptize both adults, who've chosen their path, and infants, whose parents have declared they will bring them up to know the grace of the Lord. I wonder sometimes if the difference between lost and found is mostly about timing – because the parable is clear the seeker never stops until the lost are found.

And we are tasked with being agents of the one who sought us, giving grace, seeking those who are in need of aid, and finding in ourselves somehow, the ability to offer the aid that is needed with kindness and humility.

What a profound calling.

What are you doing about it? A few weeks ago, the faithful remnant who were here on Labor Day had the experience of watching me squirm on the hook as I considered the implications of a story for your clergy. But now it is my turn to return the favor and ask you plainly, if grace is real, what are you doing about it?

Which brings me to the final vantage point from which to consider this parable, which is the vantage point of being *in the way*.

Nothing would please me more than to say that the church is never, ever in the way of grace. It would please me, but it would not be true and you would know it, because the condition of being simultaneously lost and found, sinner and saint, means that we aren't perfect and consequently, our attempts to mediate grace might just wind up well, being in the way of God. Again, Niebuhr reminds us we sin in our best deeds as well as our worst. That could be seen as a pessimistic way to look at things.

Think about it this way. David Brooks wrote an op-ed piece in the New York Times entitled *The Gospel of Wealth* and it gets to the heart of it.

I'm going to grossly simplify what he said. Brooks said when our economy got overheated, we lost our minds and we bought everything too big, too bright, too flashy and too much. And in the bust, we've actually gained clarity. Working to further this clarity is a minister named David Platt. Platt is a pastor who served a megachurch and drew the determination that perhaps a large part of the problem churches face in mediating grace is the culture of large itself. Brooks cites him, "Americans have built themselves multi-million-dollar worship palaces, he argues. These have become like corporations, competing for market share by offering social centers, child-care programs, first class entertainment and comfortable, consumer Christianity. Jesus, Platt notes, made it hard on his followers. He created a minichurch, not a mega one. Today, however, building budgets dwarf charitable budgets, and Jesus is portrayed as a genial suburban dude. 'When we gather in our church building to sing and lift up our hands in worship, we may not actually be worshipping the Jesus of the Bible, instead we may be worshipping ourselves.'"[21]

That's not really our schtick here, but what Brooks is talking about is actually much subtler. He's talking making idols out of particular visions and losing sight of what God is calling us to do.

So let me repeat the question: if grace is real, what are you doing about it?

You see, when Jesus told these stories, it was to the Pharisees. Those poor Pharisees, they've been so maligned, and I'm being quite serious. They weren't trying to be difficult… in fact the very fact that they are so often Jesus' conversation partners indicate to some that they were perhaps the

---

[21] David Brooks. *The Gospel of Wealth* in the *New York Times*. 09-07-2010

closest conversation partners Jesus had… they wanted to be good, wanted to live faithfully and they wanted to know why Jesus was associating with sinners! It's plenty easy to malign them and lump them in with exactly the sort of scenario Brooks describes, but it wouldn't be accurate any more than it would be fair to sit here and judge the faith of those who worship at the megachurches Platt is challenging. The point is the Pharisees are faithfully trying to be faithful and in the process… they got in the way. So do we all sometimes.

It's painfully easy to be in the way of grace. It just takes one thing: assuming that our mind is the mind of God and our ways are the ways of God. We have to test our vision – as a church and on our own.

Faithful living means that we need to be ahead of the curve of culture, not behind it, not reacting to circumstances pedantically pedaling moralism like those maligned Pharisees, but instead daring to risk being open to God's leading. The stories of grace we encountered this morning about lostness and foundness and our fundamental inability to make ourselves one or the other but only to live in grace and seek to share that grace as widely and inclusively as possible are but a reminder of the calling God has given us.

And we have to *do* something about it.

German theologian Helmut Thielicke claimed that the calling of the Christian is to risk heresy in the sharing of a grace as wide as God's love. The function of the church is to be the needle on the compass of culture pointing toward grace. That's our calling, and it's not easy because it requires constantly pushing our own self-imposed perceptions of lostness and foundness in order to respond to the needs of the world for grace. That is what the church is here to do, to tell the story of grace and the point the way to it.

In the name of the Father, and of the Son, and of the Holy Ghost, Amen.

Do Not Be Weary
2 Thessalonians 3:6-13; Luke 21:5-19

Years ago, my brother was flying to Las Vegas for a training course and he and several physicians were traveling together. As the plane prepared to board they called the first-class passengers to board and one of his colleagues stood up to walk toward the plane. "Tom," my brother said, "Aren't you booked with the rest of us?"

His colleague, who is a tall man, answered, "You all can ride in the back with the chickens if you want, but you can't seriously think I'm flying all the way to Vegas with my knees crammed up against my elbows."

I thought of that as I read Frank Bruni's column in the New York Times this past week.[22]

In years gone by, if you were tall, you either flew first class, or arrived early to the airport gambling that a kindly ticket agent would place you in the exit row seating where you might pass your flight without feeling like a pretzel. But now you can buy that privilege. For an extra premium over the price of the flight we can spring for extra and purchase the right to fling the emergency exit hatch off the side of the plane and help our fellow passengers down the inflatable chute. We will pay for that privilege for an extra six inches of legroom.

And I'm not judging you if you do, just so we're clear. I've sat crammed against the bulkhead enough times that I can't definitely say what I wouldn't do to extend my legs fully during a trans-Atlantic flight, and I'm not even six feet tall.

But, Bruni says, by monetizing it, attaching value to it, or making it a perk that comes with airline status, we've turned it into something else. It's now a marker of value.

He writes, "Lately, the places and ways in which Americans are economically segregated are popping up everywhere. The plane mirrors the sports arena (I am just barely suppressing my opinion about the Braves here), the theater, the gym."

---

[22] Frank Bruni. *The Extra Legroom Society*, in *The New York Times*. 11/12/2013

I was shocked. There can't seriously be class stratification at the gym?

He went on, "No sooner does a fitness trend appear than it spawns strata, so that you can spin in candlelight at SoulCycle, in less gilded trappings at Crunch, or in bare-bones fashion at the YMCA. There's an accordant price scale. Even the fanciest gyms have rungs of enhanced fanciness, such as executive locker rooms. At Equinox, trainers are designated by numbers – tiers 1, 2, and 3 – that signal their experience and hourly rate, and there are deluxe inner sanctums within certain Equinox clubs. They use eye-scanning technology to figure out who belongs."

He went on to talk about our Hertz status, our Delta level, and our insurance plan level as well as the ability to purchase the ability at theme parks to step in front of other, waiting patrons to go on a ride.

How utterly and completely exhausting!

Seriously, I thought about what it takes to achieve such status and of course, I know your smartphone will track it all for you – I have stayed at some fine hotels on points, after all, but very thought of what it takes to accrue all of those advantages, let alone the means of monitoring them, left me all but exhausted.

I wonder sometimes if exhaustion is not one of the greatest challenges facing culture and the church today. I listen to some of what particularly our young families here at the church have to juggle in order to make life work and it makes me tired on their behalves.

Indeed, a while back I debated asking Melinda to have a banner printed up to place on the street out on Morningside Drive that read simply, "Come sit an hour and do just one thing, 11 a.m. on Sundays."

Constant activity strikes me at times as a perverse way of seeing value and a strident means of managing life.

Of course, I am quickly told and rightly so that this is the way the world works today. This is the reality of life. The fact that the 1-85/1-285 interchange is perfectly capable of depriving me of an hour of my life should I be so misfortunate as to be there at 4:30 in the afternoon is immutable. It doesn't matter if I don't like it or if I rail against the stupidity of placing that many cars only a mere 12 lanes at one time – *it doesn't change.*

That's life. That's the reality we've been dealt, or the reality we've dealt ourselves and it isn't going anywhere, just like me if I'm sitting on the highway that time of day. Pretending otherwise is foolish. It's not changing.

But surely it is exhausting sometimes?

I read this week that the National Institutes of Health reports that one in five Americans is living with fatigue that is so severe that it interferes with daily normal life.

Fatigue can lead to depression, irritability and a generally negative outlook on life. This is no secret.

And yet the apostle writes to the Thessalonians, to us, "Do not be weary."

It could seem a bit tone deaf, couldn't it?

Surely women and men worked as hard then as they do now?

And yet there are more people I know than not who are working very hard, for long hours, who are energized, happy and enthusiastic about what they are doing.

And there are still others who muddle through, but don't find their labors to be onerous.

It reminds me of a woman with whom I worked many years ago, Joan, who would regularly admonish me to take my day off. If she saw me in the church, she wanted to know why. If I returned e-mail on Friday, she would reply saying, "That is well and good, but I'm not even going to read this until tomorrow because you are OFF today!"

And she worked more hours than I could count.

I asked her once, "Joan, how is it that you, who admonish me regularly to take a break are working so many hours. You wake at 4:30 so you can be in the gym by 5, at the office by 6:30 and you don't go home until late in the evening. And yet, you are worried about *me* burning out!?"

She replied, "I like it. First, note that I always take my day off, Saturday, as a day of Sabbath. Second, I firmly believe that when you are doing work that you find deeply meaningful and that brings you joy, you will not burn out."

I have wondered through the years whether she is right.

As I have moved in ministry through different roles I have certainly noted the times when the hours grew later and later, when I, and others, have departed from the church in the dark to drive home. And I do think she is on to something. When the work we are doing matters, when we know it matters, we may be tired without being exhausted.

Vocation is doing that work that brings our labors into alignment with God's hopes. Perhaps it is easier to keep it going when our labors are living into God's hopes.

If you think *calling* is just for preachers, it's not.

God calls all of us to work for the kingdom – some of us are fortunate to do it for pay. Many of us find that place where our labors align with God's hope in another place.

For many years, my father worked in a job that he didn't like very much because it paid very well. I'm grateful that he shifted toward the end of his career to something he enjoyed more, but he will quickly tell you that the years that he worked at the job that he didn't love were not wasted. "It was a means to an end," he would say. "I loved what it enabled me to do – to take time off and be with my family."

The overwhelming evidence suggests that when labors have rewards they are more easily sustained. When we see the value in what we are doing, whether it is for the purpose of helping a client, healing the sick, preaching the Gospel, teaching a child, paying the tuition, it makes it easier. It has meaning. It becomes sustainable.

It is easier not to be weary.

But what are we to make of Paul's words, "Anyone unwilling to work should not eat."

It is not a political statement. Paul is not writing about minimum wage or right to work laws. He is pragmatic to the core. This is about a particular problem.

And yet, it sounds vaguely unchristian. Or maybe it sounds explicitly unchristian.

In the Christian faith, this is not how we assign value.

That sounds a different from, "Aligning our labors with God's hopes," doesn't it?

As is generally the case, Paul is writing to a specific problem in the church in Thessalonica.

At a glance, it seems as simple as the line suggests: some are not working. They should be, therefore let them have a little hunger therapy to motivate some action.

But it turns out it's a bit more than that.

We read this morning from Luke's Gospel about the day of the Lord. That's a recurring Biblical theme. You'll find it all over the Gospels and you'll also find it in the Hebrew Scriptures, the Old Testament. It goes deep.

There is throughout the pages of scripture the theme that God's work is unfinished, and that one day, when it is all said and done, the work of God will be concluded.

That's a big day. That is the day of the Lord. And there are all sorts of imagery attached to it. One of the beautiful spirituals in our hymnal sings, "When the stars begin to fall…"

There are all sorts of imagery associated with the day of the Lord, but it all points to a nexus where it all comes together, where God's vision of creation and the reality of existence come together and it is God's shalom.

It's a wonderful image and it turns out that some of the Thessalonian Christians were convinced, absolutely convinced, that this would happen right after lunch. Or breakfast. Or while they were in the shower. They thought it was imminent and so they wanted to be ready.

So they quit work.

And they quit working.

And yet the day of the Lord didn't happen after lunch… or breakfast… or while they were in the shower. Day after day, it didn't happen.

And with all of this non-work, they got bored.

And then they got to meddling. They didn't have anything else to do, so they would spend their days as unofficial supervisors of others' work.

There are few things as irritating as an unofficial supervisor, don't you think?

And to them Paul wrote, "That is enough. There is work to be done. If you don't want to get on with it, fine, get out of it, leave us alone."

That's when work doesn't matter – when it becomes meaningless.

But work does matter. It is meaningful. There is the possibility of using our labors for the good of the world. We can align our labors with God's hopes.

There was a cartoon I saw a number of years back, it was a memo. It read, "Jesus is coming. Look busy."

The simple truth is that Jesus probably isn't coming after lunch today.

I'm not going to rule it out, but in this instance, past performance does seem to indicate future expectations. I wouldn't count on it.

And yet, throughout his writings, Paul seemed to do just that, to count on Jesus' return any day. And even with his hope and expectation of just that, he kept working. He admonished the others to keep working. "Do not be weary in doing what is right," he said.

Do not be weary of doing what is right because that is the way that God is working in the world.

I read another article this week, this time, on NPR, by Matt De La Pena.

I'd never heard of him, but he is an author of adolescent fiction. Yet, it was not always a foregone conclusion that his life would follow this path. Reading books was for the sensitive. In his own words, "If there was one thing a guy couldn't be in the my *machista*, Mexican family, it was sensitive."[23]

It all changed when a professor, his sophomore year, handed him a novel and asked him to read it. Sometime before he graduated – it didn't matter when – and then come to her and discuss it. He read it slowly at first. And then he

---

[23] Matt De La Pena. *Sometimes the 'Tough Teen" is Quietly Writing Stories*. NPR.com 11/11/13

devoured it. As he finished the final paragraphs, the tough guy fought back tears.

The novel was The Color Purple. And she said what she loved best was that even in the harshest and ugliest of circumstances, there is still hope. He decided that was what he loved best.

It was a moment of redemption with deep repercussions. We don't ever give up hope in this world while we are waiting on the world to come.

Yes, we are waiting on Jesus. But the work we are doing now matters. There is an old piece of rabbinical wisdom that suggests that God left creation a little bit undone so that we might be allowed to participate with God in creating something that brings about God's shalom. Do not be weary of doing what is right. Do not be weary.

In the name of the Father, and of the Son, and of the Holy Ghost, Amen.

The Mystery of God
Isaiah 58:1-12; 1 Corinthians 2:1-16

I have to confess that it seems to me that we are running at a bit of a high rate of volatility these days. For myriad reasons, particular to each individual, the news is a risky show to watch. It's risky because you don't know what you're going to see – it might be a heart-warming story of shared humanity, or it could just as easily be two senators about to bludgeon one another to death with words. When the world gets so hot under the collar, one has to wonder whether our elected officials are something between the boy-scout troop leaders they seem to present themselves to be or rather something more akin to gladiators intent on fighting to the death.

But the simple truth of the matter is that today is no more or less unique as yesterday and as will be tomorrow. Whatever it is today, something will be forthcoming tomorrow.

Which I suppose is another way of saying, "wherever you go, there you are." But I have no doubt that for all of us the ups and downs of any week are indeed personal and particular, as is every day, as is every minute.

That is the only way that any of us ever encounter the Word of God: personally and particularly.

True, we gather and read it together. True, together we rule out the more hare-brained interpretations, but there's no getting around the fact that you will hear the word of God as *you* today, and I'll hear it as *me*, and we'll hear it with our own politics, our own likes and dislikes, fears and phobias. How could it be otherwise? We are each ourselves!

As for me, when I turned to the lectionary text, carrying with me all of my particularity, one phrase of the letter to the Corinthians jumped out. As I turned to the first letter to the Corinthians, I fixed on the *mystery* of God.

Now, I actually find the mystery of God quite comforting – that there is a great fullness self of God that is not known to me – it makes it less intimidating to admit that I don't know what I don't know, indeed, it actually comforts me to think there is more going on than meets the eye – think of the hymns we sing that wrap us in the expansiveness of God – of the Father's love begotten, ere all worlds began to be… evermore and evermore…

There's just something wonderful sometimes about knowing you don't have to know it all, indeed that it is impossible to know it all.

But that brings me to the rub: despite the mysteries of God – all that we cannot understand, there is a very great deal that we do understand, that we can wrap our heads around. Indeed, one of my seminary professors years ago cautioned my classmates and me against, as he said, "running up the flag of mystery too soon."

There are things that we do know about God. We know what God has already revealed about God's self.

You know that great old Maya Angelou quote, "When someone shows you who they are, believe them the first time"? Well, it happens that rule of thumb applies to God as well. When God shows you who God is, believe it.

Some time back, I guess it's been a few months or a year or so, I remember telling you all about a favorite cartoon of mine in the New Yorker. Actually, I have several, but this particular one is trade-specific.

A robed and collared minister is shaking hands at the doorway of a majestic church on a Sunday morning in the background. In the foreground, a man who looked much like the monopoly man and his equally plutocratic wife were making their way toward their Rolls-Royce where the chauffeur was waiting to open the door. The caption read, "you know, it can't be easy for him not to offend us."

Well, I relayed this story to you, and we chuckled over it because you knew perfectly well that I was going to then try to lower the boom.

After church, a couple of you said to me, "Oh, Baron, you could never offend us."

Now, that could be taken a few different ways, you know?

On the one hand, it could be assumed that this couple was so worldly that nothing that would come out of my mouth could possibly offend.

Or it could mean that my affect and demeanor are so truly unflappable that everyone, in turn, around me has to wonder whether or not I really meant what I just said.

Or, it could mean I'm so diplomatic that I can tell you where to go and make you believe you'd enjoy the trip. I hope what it means is that we've done the work of community and relationship building that means we can speak honestly with one another.

Whatever the meaning, I was told that I couldn't offend you.

Well, I'm going to give it the good old college try again.

I'm not going out of my way to step on toes, but I am unabashedly going to share what the Bible says. That, with the ethical claims of Jesus Christ, may very well stand in opposition to what many of us believe about how the world should work. Almost to a person, that should shake us down to the foundations.

We read two of them already today.

I don't want to hide behind the words, so let's see if I can just say them plainly.

God is now, has always been, and if the Bible is reliable, will always be on the side of refugees.

God has shown who God is – and it is up to us to believe it.

Slow down over those words in Isaiah again, as God tells us what God wants from us:

"Is such the fast that I choose, a day to humble oneself? Is it to bow down the head like a bulrush, and to lie in sackcloth and ashes? Will you call *this* a fast, a day acceptable to the LORD? *Is* not *this* the fast that I choose: to lose the bonds of injustice, to undo the thongs of the yoke, to let the oppressed go free, and to break every yoke? Is it not to share your bread with the hungry, and bring the homeless poor into your house; when you see the naked, to cover them, and not to hide yourself from your own kin?"

God has shown who God is. God has shown what God values. Let there be absolutely no mistake about it: God is on the side of the refugees. And if we want to be on the same side as God, we have to be on the side of the refugees as well.

God is reliable. The God we worship in this unique moment is the God who was breathed into those words when they were spoken from the lips of God's prophet.

Now maybe that doesn't offend you – but remember this: when it comes to God and what God wants from us, we know. God has told us. We know, and that knowledge is relentless. What's more, this idea that God will be on the side of the poor, the marginalized, the oppressed and the refugee is not a fleeting idea in the Old Testament.

Do you remember the sin of Sodom?

Everybody associates Sodom and Gomorrah, two ancient cities, with a clobber text that is erroneously used to malign LGBT people. But here's what the prophet Ezekiel had to say: "This was the guilt of your sister Sodom: she and her daughters had arrogance, abundant food and careless ease, but she did not help the poor and needy."

And of course, there's Amos, where God declares to hate, to despise the solemn assemblies of the people – but who in turn encourages all who are doing justice. And of course, Micah: doing justice, loving kindness and living humbly with God.

I could go on for days like this, really I could, because the fundamental value of Bible is the enduring humanity of the people, who are made in God's image; and the demand of God that everyone made in God's image be concerned with lifting up the others around them to the same image and stature.

So that's our first offensive ethical claim of the Gospel: if you want to be on God's side, you have to be on the side of the refugee, the poor, the hungry and the marginalized. Not just philosophically, but practically and tangibly.

In fact, let me put a fine point on it with the words of Paul Hansen,

"In a community where those who regarded themselves as the most religious had converted religion into private acts of study and ritual thereby leaving the entire realm of social relations and commerce under the dominion of ruthless, self-serving exploitation, the prophet reaffirms the classical understanding of Yahwism… it is a rigorously moral understanding that places the one who would be true to God on the side of the same one whom God reached out to help and empower, those suffering injustice at the hands of the authorities; those imprisoned for acts of conscience, those denied their fair share of the land's produce, those denied housing and proper clothing, those turned away even by their own relatives. The appeal is an impassioned one to the heart of the community. It is a plea to reclaim authentic humanity by replacing cold, calculating self-interest with acts of loving-kindness that restore genuine communal solidarity."[24]

Human beings are free moral agents. We can be on anybody's side we choose. But if we want to be on God's side, we better choose the poor.

Now, for those of you who aren't offended yet, don't worry, there's more.

However, much I may have wanted to hear the mysteries of God – to luxuriate in a God so big as to be anything, God has shown us who God is with reference to that as well.

Which is why Paul says to the Corinthians, "I could have taught you with the mystery of God, but instead I have determined to know only Christ, and Christ crucified.

To preach "Christ crucified" is to remember that even the resurrection does not remove the imprint of the cross from Jesus Christ. To know "Christ and him crucified" is to know the depth and width and breadth of God's love even – especially – for the oppressor and the enemy.

Indeed, to borrow from Karl Barth, the cross is the crisis of human history whose ripples go out into all eternity.

Which is to say that there is no avenue, no individual untouched by the redemptive work of God. There is no avenue, no individual untouched by the love of God. And we are, in turn, made in God's image, called to love the enemy and the oppressor as even our very own selves.

And Christ knows that we will fail at that not once or twice, but a great many times, therefore standing in need of God's mercy and grace ourselves.

And it is because God wants more for humankind than awkward family dinners. Because if you weren't offended by the suggestion that to be on God's side you must be on the side of the poor, great. That means you have a Biblical understanding of the economy of God. But perhaps you might be

---

[24] Paul D. Hanson, *Isaiah 40-66* in *Interpretation,* Mays, Miller, Achetemeier, eds. (John Knox Press: Louisville, 1995) pp 205-206

offended to learn the seating chart of the kingdom of heaven and to know with whom you will be spending eternity at table in the kingdom.

God always takes the long view of creation, looking not at what is, but at what can yet be. God always takes the long view of you and me, looking not only at what is, but at what can yet be.

There is a story I love – I shared it with the Session at our retreat last Saturday. It's a bit of old rabbinical wisdom. The story goes that two brothers were in same business milling wheat. They worked hard, the business grew profitable and eventually they were able to realize their investments, so they each built silos to hold their wheat.

Only one day, the older brother became very thoughtful. He thought to himself, "This is not just. We take equal shares of the family business, but I have a wife and children. God has so richly blessed me, and my poor brother doesn't have the comforts of family, of a wife and child. It's little enough, but I should share my wheat." And under the cover of darkness, he began, nightly, to transfer some of his wealth to his brother.

Meanwhile the younger brother began to think to himself, "This is not right. This is not just. My brother has a wife and child to support beyond himself. And here we are, paying us both the same dividend as though our needs were the same. It is little enough, but let me return to my brother what should be his by needs." And under the cover of darkness, he began to shift wealth to his brother. Each marveled every morning how their stockpiles never seemed to diminish.

Inevitably, one night they met, and with tears and great joy each realized the sacrifice of the other, each heard of the love of the other. And the rabbis say that, in that moment, God said, "This is where my temple shall be built, so that my house may always be a place of joyful union and reunion."

And dear friends, we are in God's house, and the table is set, with a place for each, enemy and oppressor, refugee and the impoverished. We are in God's house, the place of joyful union and reunion, and the table is set with a place for all.

In the name of the Father, and of the Son, and of the Holy Ghost, Amen.

Part Three

Vocation: Our Common Calling

Abounding in Hope
Romans 15:4-13; Matthew 3:1-12

Perhaps you remember The Worst Case Scenario Survival Handbook?

It was a popular Christmas gift and stocking-stuffer around the holidays in the year 2000. I'm not sure what prompted it, but I remember it being pretty wildly popular in Indianapolis. The original edition included instructions for such things as landing an airplane, surviving a shark-attack, and other such scenarios.

The authors went on to write survival guides for travel – I can understand that one, college – also, a tough time for many folks, and weddings – I could have used that one a time or twelve. But the series was probably approaching its sell-by date when the authors wrote a Worst Case Scenario Survival Handbook for Golf.

I suppose there are certain eras that lend themselves to a bit of gallows humor about impending doom. Surely such an era would have been John the Baptist's world. His world was characterized by a foreign occupation with a pretender-King married to a harlot on the throne. I suspect John the Baptist could have written the worst case scenario survivor guide for the first century, until, of course, his untimely demise.

Certain eras lend themselves to pessimism. But that wasn't John's message!

He came preaching, "Repent!" and that is a hopeful word. It's a hopeful word because it says, "turn around, go a different direction, it doesn't have to be the worst case scenario. You don't have to live this way." John would have known what the word meant. He would have known you don't go around yelling "repent" at those who have no hope.

Paul's era would have lent itself to a certain amount of pessimism as well.

Here are a few reasons Paul might be pessimistic: "Imprisonments," he said, "with countless floggings, and often near death. Five times I have received from the Jews the forty lashes minus one. Three times I was beaten with rods. Once I received a stoning. Three times I was shipwrecked; for a night and a day I was adrift at sea; on frequent journeys, in danger from rivers, danger from bandits, danger from my own people, danger from Gentiles, danger in the city, danger in the wilderness, danger at sea, danger from false brothers and sisters; in toil and hardship, through many a sleepless night, hungry and thirsty, often without food, cold and naked."[25]

And yet, here in the fifteenth chapter of Romans, we find, not a sonnet to suffering, but rather the opposite: a homily of hope.

The epistle, or letter, to the Romans is Paul's crack at a systematic theology. And at its crowning moment, before he moves to the closing business, the housekeeping matters he has to deal with, he ends with message for us to *abound in hope.*

And for Paul, this is not a generic hope. It is a specific hope, rooted in the unity of creation in Jesus Christ. As one New Testament scholar notes:

"The goal of God's act of grace in Jesus Christ is therefore unity among his creatures, a unity which…is to become reality in the present in the community of those who acknowledge God's gracious lordship in Christ. If the universal scope of the mutual welcome of all peoples are to extend to one another waits until the restoration of creation, with its new heaven and new earth, that mutual welcome is nevertheless already to be visible reality within the church."[26]

Remember, Paul is writing to the church in its earliest, formative stages, and his message to those believers and to us is that whatever is going on out there – whatever worst case scenario may unfold, we are Christians first, foremost, and together, in order that we may abound in hope for the world around us.

He has three activities by which we abound in hope.

We are to 1) live in harmony, 2) glorify God, and 3) welcome one another.

We are called to live in harmony. Well now. Just who is this "we?"

It is the church. It is an offense against the Gospel when the church fights against itself. So much so was this a concern that even the reformers who led the establishment of alternative churches to the Roman milieu had deeply stringent criteria for what constituted a justifiable break with one another. For Calvin, for the Scot's Confession, the markers of the true church were that the Word must be rightly proclaimed and the sacraments rightly

---

[25] 2 Corinthians 11:16-33
[26] Paul Achtemeier, *Romans* in *Interpretation*, Mays, Miller and Achtemeier, eds. (John Knox Press: Atlanta, 1985) p 225

administered. No matter what else might be going wrong, if these two things were right, there was no justification to break up.

That's instructive. I have deeply critical things to say about certain aspects of the universal Church's life together. I am critical of the sexism and homophobia of one part of the church. I am deeply critical of any portion of the church that marches in lockstep with a political establishment. But my criticism must be tempered – indeed, all of our criticisms, must be tempered by the reality that it is an argument in the family. We are, after all, the Communion of the Saints. Catholic theologian Hans Kung puts this well.

Writing of the communion of the saints, he says, "This is just another way of describing the church. These 'saints' are anything but exalted ideal figures. What is meant are saints without haloes: believers who still have their failings and sins yet who through God's call in Christ have foresworn the sinful world and are attempting in everyday life, for better or for worse, to follow the way of Christ's disciples."[27]

I suppose that's good news for everyone who, like me, views one or two of our fellow Christians as slightly less than haloed. Kung goes on:

"These, then, are no self-made saints, but are only 'called to be saints' (1 Cor. 1.2), 'saints in Christ Jesus' (Phil. 1.1.), holy and beloved elect (Col.3.12). So the church may be called 'holy' only to the degree that it is called by God himself through Christ in the Spirit as the community of believers and has placed itself at his service, raised above the banality of the world's course by God's liberating concern."[28]

In other words, God called all of those other Christians just exactly the same way God called us: through Jesus Christ, and we're stuck in this messy reality called the church, and by our harmony, we show hope to the world. Whatever we have to say, we are Christian first.

We are called to glorify God.

This one, also, is simultaneously easy and difficult. It's easy to say the right words about God and what God has done in Jesus Christ. Indeed, scores of generations of Christians memorized the Shorter Catechism, which begins

---

[27] Hans Kung, *Credo: The Apostles' Creed Explained for Today.* (Doubleday: NY, 1993) p 141
[28] Ibid.

with the words, "What is the chief end of humankind?" The answer is, "To glorify God and enjoy God forever."

It's written into our DNA that we are to praise and glorify God. Indeed, though the Catechism itself will go on to express that activity in exclusively Christian terms, the *universal* call of humankind is to glorify God. That's what we're made for. That's why we need to worship, and to be *in* worship.

But it's easy to get the words right and the meaning wrong.

Perhaps you've seen Tyler Perry's *Madea Goes to Jail*. Yes, I know we're risking whiplash switching from Hans Kung to Mabel Simmons, but stay with me. Now, if you know the movie, you know that it begins with Madea "correcting" a would-be car-jacker by taking him on an insane joyride. Afterwards she is hauled before Judge Mablean and she attempts to present herself as a model citizen, spouting endless, meaningless God-talk. "If the Lord gets me out of this, I'm goin' by the church," she says, as she approaches the witness stand.

Standing before the judge she says, "You ain't got to say nothing, I am living for the Lort, Halleujer, I feel him in my spirit, you know as I think about the goodness of Jesus, and all he has done for me, my soul cries out 'hallelujer' thank God for saving me."

After being ordered to anger-management therapy with Dr. Phil, she violates her probation and is subsequently hauled off to jail where the God-talk becomes meaningful. Being confronted with her own situation, hearing others describe their situation as somebody else's fault, something within her snaps and launches into a tirade about personal responsibility and change.

That's meaningful God-talk. That's the God-talk that doesn't make grace cheap, but that gives glory to God: recognition of the goodness of God shown to us in the redemptive work of Jesus Christ. That's glorifying God. Don't say it if doesn't mean anything, but when it does, don't hold back. Because when it comes to knowing our place before God, we are Christians first then as well.

Finally, **we are called to welcome one another.**

If there is one thing I don't worry about with this congregation, it is understanding the meaning of the word *welcome*. I have heard the leaders of this congregation wrestle with thorny issues, including even our own child protection policy, and it is one of my moments of almost sinful pride in the leadership of this church that they did so from the standpoint of what it means for us to have been welcomed in Christ. I don't need to say much about this one, but remember this: a welcome that is an inch deep and a mile wide isn't much of a welcome, whether that's in our homes, our offices, our schools, our day-care centers, our parks, our streets and with our most obnoxious neighbors. We welcome as Christ has welcomed us. It is a hallmark of *abounding in hope* that our words of welcome are genuine, deep and durable. Because in our welcome also, we are Christians first and foremost.

We are called to live in harmony, to glorify God, and to welcome one another because *our hope* isn't the end-game. It is the hope of the world that is the end-game. I'm reminded of a story Fred Craddock told many years ago about how he was in Los Angeles for the annual meeting of the Society of Biblical Literature. It's a great organization, they talk about important stuff – you know, it's through good scholarship, good rigorous study of the Bible that the church has made some of its most important advances, from rejecting slavery, to recognizing the leadership of women, to understanding that God's hospitality is for everyone – including the LGBT community – all because of good, rigorous, hard thinking.

But Craddock was at the gathering of the Society of Biblical Literature, and he was walking through the hotel lobby and he was stopped by a rather plain looking woman of about forty, who asked him, "Are you here with the Bible people?"

"Yes," he replied.

"Are the sessions open to anyone," she wanted to know?

"Some are," he said.

"Well, I want to come."

"Why?" he asked.

"Because I've been walking the streets of Los Angeles since I was sixteen years old making a mess of my life, and the other night I caught my daughter beginning the same life. I want to become a Christian." Craddock said she had an old Bible, the kind with a zipper. He unzipped it and marked some passages for her, and then he called the minister of a local church, who came, and they met together and finally went off together.

Craddock concluded, some people might say, "See all the foolishness of Scholarly meetings?" But he said no, it is by understanding our faith that we come to understand our place in it.[29]

In the world, whether full of pessimism or optimism, we are called to be Christians first, abounding in hope, living together in harmony, glorifying God, and welcoming one another, because it is in the abounding of hope in ourselves that we show *hope* to the world.

In the name of the Father, and of the Son, and of the Holy Ghost, Amen.

---

[29] Fred Craddock. *Craddock Stories*, Graves and Ward, eds. (Chalice Press: St. Louis, 2001) p 129

Basic Good Advice
Romans 13:8-14; Matthew 18:15-20

In an article entitled *Six Stories of Sin*, Brian Doyle recounts confessions made to parish pastors or priests. A few do seem a bit shy of the mark – here's one confession:

"The admission of assault (but not battery) on a squirrel…by a home owner, occasioned by what the home owner characterized as 'Continual, deliberate provocation' by the squirrel in question, upon which the home owner's temper finally snapped, and he did roar at, threaten, insult, denigrate and impugn the squirrel, about which the home owner felt awful later."

Another was the sin of running up the score of a little league game because one of the coaches had once dated and rather unceremoniously dumped the wife of the other coach. Faced with the opportunity to avenge his wife's offense, the coach told his team to apply the full-court press despite the team being up by 24 points. The coach felt guilty the next day and sought the counsel of the priest, who asked him if he'd like to confess. The coach replied, "Well, no. We only won by 32. That's not a sin – winning by 50 would have been a sin."[30]

That's not really sin, is it?

And then there are the times when there is no mal-intention. just thoughtlessness. I am in mind of a time my friend Sally was seated with her back to the door of a restaurant during a cold snap, and each time the door would swing open, she'd brace herself for the cold blast. Finally, the door stayed open and she reflexively said, loudly, "CLOSE THE DOOR," only to turn around and see that the very elderly lady coming into the restaurant had gotten the wheel of her oxygen tank caught on the doorframe.

Then there was the time when I was having such a rotten day and I'd gone to Brooks Brothers to buy some pants and when I had to buy the larger size was so utterly rude to the clerk that I didn't even make it to the car before I knew I had to go back to the store and apologize.

Any one of us can, if we are honest, remember a time when we know we should have acted better. We can remember a time when we could have acted

---

[30] Brian Doyle in *The Christian Century* July 23, 2014

better. That's only one of a multitude of reasons why I do not have a fish on the trunk of my car... I'd constantly have to apologize.

We all know when we should have done better.

We all know when we need to confess our sin – I appreciate the honesty of those of you who tell us that we don't leave enough time between the corporate confession and assurance of pardon... I appreciate the honesty it takes to admit that we're already passing the peace and you're not yet gotten through Tuesday's confession.

This is all well and good, but what about when the equation reverses? What about when you're the wronged party?

And what about when it really matters?

It's fine to laugh and chuckle about slapstick sins, but what about when it really matters, when you're the one who is hurt to the core, when you're not a hundred percent sure you even want to reconcile what is wrong?

How hard is it then to follow Jesus' commandment?

This is basic good advice for resolving differences.

And it is advice that most of us won't ever actually follow.

Look at what he says: If someone sins against you, you have to tell them.

I don't know about you, but I'm not inclined to tell someone if they hurt my feelings. I'm much more inclined to stew about it.

We might even be inclined to talk about it too – to other people.

Edwin Friedman calls this triangulation. Don't tell the person who hurt your feelings, tell someone else and then you expect them to tell the person who hurt your feelings and it's all handled behind the scenes.

If someone sins against you – tell them when it is just the two of you.

Don't gossip about it.

Don't bring in a third party.

Don't simmer and seethe. Tell the truth.

That's so hard to do. But if you do it, Jesus says, that one is regained. Community is preserved. I wish I could tell you that I have a perfect track record on this, but I don't. Maybe you don't either. We should take note for ourselves.

Only after step one can we go to step two.

Step two is when another person goes with you to deal with the sin. And note that it is not triangulation, it's still direct communication. If someone has hurt you, you still have to tell them.

Then comes stage three. This the stage where the whole church gets involved. I have to confess this seems impracticable to me at this point, and it's not just because I'm the pastor and I know I'm going to have to listen to it all if we go down this road, and I'm a little afraid that it's going to read a little like the story of six sins with which we started today.

There's a difference between annoying and irritating someone and sinning against them.

Annoying someone is just that. It's grit in the gears. It's personalities not jiving. It's differences of opinion on things that sometimes matter a great deal but at the end of the day it's still just opinion.

Sin is different. Sin is brokenness.

If you annoy me, I'm probably not going to tell you. If I annoy you, I probably don't need to hear about it.

But if the relationship between us is broken, we have a responsibility to address it. If the relationship between you and your child is broken, it needs to be addressed. If the relationship between you and the person you share your life with is broken, it needs to be addressed. God does not want us to persist in brokenness. And brokenness is the path of least resistance. That's why it's so pernicious. That's why Jesus knows how deadly it is to remain in sin. Because sin is brokenness and sin causes brokenness.

Sin caused Ferguson.

Sin caused ISIS.

Sin caused that in your life that you don't want to name but you know is not right, and mine too.

We can't live in brokenness.

Not all resolutions are neat and clean. Not all resolutions are happy. But the idea of continuing in brokenness runs counter to the wholeness that God wants for us.

God wants us to be whole. God wants that for us individually, and God wants that for communities.

It's the most extraordinary basic good advice that most of us won't follow…but it's not just advice… it's a command.

What Jesus is commanding is community. It's real community, not just associations, and nice acquaintanceship, but real and deep community that cares for the fabric of creation in a way that drafts us into God's creative and redemptive activity.

It is also costly. If you follow Jesus' command, it is going to cost you. It exacts a cost to tell the truth when we don't want to.

You know, there's a real difference between what is expensive and what is costly. What is expensive may or may not be worth much. My car's expensive, but at the end of the day, it's not worth a thing other than money.

But real relationships where truth is told and burdens are shared – that's costly. That's worth something. Real relationships where when the world comes crashing in those sisters and brothers will be there – that's important. That's costly. That's worth the discomfort and unease of telling the truth.

There's one last thing Jesus said about this – he said if those steps don't work, let the sinner be like a tax collector or a gentile to you.

That sounds so harsh, and surely it is. I don't know if he knew that most of us won't get to that point with someone – we'll give up far sooner than that – but here's the thing for us to remember – Jesus had a real thing for tax collectors and gentiles. He kept sharing meals with them. So when you've exhausted Jesus' teachings on the one who has sinned against you, just remember that Jesus isn't exhausted yet.

And that is good news. That is the promise of the Gospel: God is never done with us. Always remember that Jesus had a thing for tax collectors and gentiles.

Forgiveness is about the most important thing that we can offer one another. It is what God has given us. And it is costly to forgive.

And forgiveness doesn't mean giving the offending party what they want. It means releasing yourself from holding that burden and relinquishing your claim to vengeance.

Elsewhere in the pages of the Bible, we read that we are not supposed to give our offering with a grudge on our hearts[31], so if you are harboring a grudge, you best let the plate go by – let the church carry the giving for you for this week. Nor are we to approach the Lord's Table for communion without examining ourselves – you can't feed a grudge from this table, so you best pass the plate on by.[32]

I have spent most of my ministry working to ensure that the church is a place of deep hospitality and welcome. I have worked for the hallmark of my ministry to be inclusivity. It matters deeply to me to know that you know that all are welcome at this table.

But I would do you a disservice today if I told you that you should come to this table and feed yourself here while you're harboring grudges.

I know many of you know the ancient Cherokee wisdom about the two wolves within each of us vying for control of our souls – the one is anger, envy, sorrow, regret, greed, arrogance, you know how it goes – and the other wolf is goodness, benevolence, generosity, truth – all of the virtues we call the fruits of the spirit. As the story culminates, the young man asks his grandfather which wolf will win.

"The one you feed," he replies.

You must deal with those who have sinned against you. Jesus has told you how.

---

[31] Matthew 5:4
[32] 1 Corinthians 11:27

The promise that I can tell you about is that this table will always be here to welcome you and your reconciled sister and brother when you return.

In the name of the Father, and of the Son, and of the Holy Ghost, Amen.

The Mustard Seed
Luke 13:18-19, Psalm 150

I'd like to tell you about my friend Frances Leete. She is, to my knowledge, still a member of the church in which I was raised, and when I was a little boy, she was the director of the cherub choir. Why the youngest choir in every church seems to be called the cherub choir is beyond me, because if you read about cherubs in the Bible, they're absolutely terrifying creatures, which come to think of it may be why they were called the cherub choir after all. My six-year-old brother was a cherub, so to speak, and at the age of three and half, I wanted to do everything he did, an affection I have gotten over. The cherub choir was not for three and half year olds, but undeterred, I memorized the first verse of *All Creatures of Our God and King* determined to change Mrs. Leete's mind. After hearing me sing it, she told my mother I really was too young.

But then the next morning, she called my mother and said, "Any child who wants to sing that much should be encouraged. I'll take him."

I learned a lesson then that I've been learning ever since: that actions have the power to affect profoundly how people see ourselves and the church and every aspect of life. I also learned that music is a powerful uniting force when people sing together.

I remember very little about being three and half years old, but I remember that.

It was, and remains for me, an experience of the kingdom of God.

I think we sometimes think that the kingdom of God always has to be an earth-shatteringly big thing, you know, angels with trumpets blasting, clouds and fire around a glowing Jesus, earthquakes, etc.

And yet Jesus tells us it is like a mustard seed.

I won't belabor the point: tiny seed, big tree, you get the picture.

The disciples were constantly looking for something with a little more splash, a little more oomph, a little more grandness, and at every turn, Jesus confounded them with the observation that the kingdom of God breaks in unexpectedly. The kingdom of God starts small – the kingdom of God is all around us, Jesus says. The kingdom is at work within us.

I called Jane a few weeks ago and asked her if there was anything in particular that she wanted me to preach about today – and while she and I did talk about it for a while, the one thing she was crystal clear about was that she didn't want me to make the sermon into a catalogue of thirty years of music ministry. And so today we won't talk about her terms as dean of the American Guild of Organists, nor will we mention the fact that faculty Yale Divinity School faculty cherry-picked her Liturgical Arts Camp to serve as a model for future applicants, or that when I asked her to record the Widor Toccata a few years ago for the youth silent auction, a complex piece she has hitherto referred to as "seven minutes of loud" she played it in five and a half minutes flat, we won't speak of her degrees from Salem, Eastman and Duke – and I'm a man of my word, I won't even mention them. I'll resist the allure of metaphor to substitute "ministry of music" with "The Kingdom of God," because, you see, I don't have to. Tiny seed, big tree; you get the picture.

When Walter Huff, the chorus master for the Atlanta Opera, retired from the church I serve in Atlanta after twenty-five years, he recounted a marvelous story of keynote address of Canadian soprano Teresa Stratas at the conference he was attending, of how she electrified him with her words about the human voice and its carrying of the divine message, and then he said, "We, in every act of life, and through our singing, as long as we are here, are messengers sent for each other: to heal each other, ourselves, and to light the way – to light the way, through our song – to light the way for everyone."

When our vocation is working through Jesus Christ the kingdom of God is apt to break in.

Vocation has come in recent years to be associated, most often, with work. But it actually derives from a very different origin. Vocation comes from the Latin root, *vocare* which means simply *to call*. When I officiate weddings, for instance, I always remind the two being married and congregation that what we're really doing is celebrating a holy calling, a vocation, into which they are entering. It's a vocation because the calling is to exemplify the love of Jesus Christ through marriage. The simplest acts become holy as they become the living of vocation.

Tiny seed, big tree; you get the picture.

I love Frederick Buechner's definition of vocation. He says, vocation is "that place where our deep gladness and the world's deep need meet."[33]

When we're living our vocation, the tiniest acts are significant.

The kingdom of God is always around us – if we'll see it. If we'll seek it – indeed, it breaks in unexpected – oftentimes at the moment we least expect it.

In her wonderful short story, *Music on the Muscatatuck*, Jessamyn West tells the story of Jess Birdwell, a devout Quaker and husband of a Quaker minister at the time of the Civil War. Birdwell lived an idyllic life on the banks of the Muscatatuck in Indiana. He has a thriving business, a loving family, a good wife. But something is missing, and soon West tells us, what is missing is music. And in the Quaker tradition, music is an idolatry, an impediment to the voice of God. As Birdwell is traveling to Philadelphia to purchase cherry trees for his nursery, he encounters a traveling organ salesman, Waldo Quigley. Quigley is a gifted salesman, with the gift of gab, as it were, and he soon has Birdwell right where he wants him. He begins talking about the organs that he sells: Payson and Clarke's, rhapsodizing about their rich, resonant sound. He cannot, of course, mimic the sound of an organ, but knowing he has a musician at heart in front of him, he improvises, singing an Irish air. West writes: "Jess said afterward that didn't have the slightest intention of making a show of himself in a B&O parlor car singing "The Old Musician and his Harp," or any other song, for that matter. But the tune was a hard thing to give the go-by; the mind already said the words, and the toe tapped the time; with the whole body already singing it, that way, opening the mouth to let the words out seemed a mighty small matter…"

Birdwell concluded his business in Philadelphia, and remembering the card of the salesman, decides to stop into a Payson and Clarke showroom and hear the music played proper. It would only be polite, after all. And so, it is that the husband of a Quaker minister finds himself the purchaser of a pump organ.

Birdwell arrives home a few days ahead of the organ, thinking he might gradually acclimate his minister wife to the idea of the instrument. It doesn't go well. He begins pontificating about how the birds sing and the angels play harps to the glory of God, and his wife astutely replies: "Thee's neither bird

---

[33] Frederick Buechner. *Wishful Thinking: A Seeker's ABC.* (HarperOne: San Francisco, 1993) p 117

nor angel, Jess Birdwell, and had the lord wanted thee, either singing or plucking a harp, there would be feathered now, one way or another."

The organ arrives. There is a husband and wife row over its arrival, and when the dust settles, the organ stays, but relegated to the attic.

It would seem that this would be well enough, except that, as it always will, rumor works its way round, and soon enough, the ministry and oversight board has come a-calling. They know their task – and it is not a pleasant one. They come in their Sunday best to the house prepared to confront their minister with her tolerant ways. And though Jess has been careful of when he has played, his young daughter, who is learning music has gone up to the attic and husband and wife alike hear the telltale sound of the bellows filling as she pumps the organ and know that what will come will tell the tale. And in that moment, Jess knows that he has sold his inheritance for a mess of potage, like Esau of the Bible, only worse: Esau only sold his birthright, Birdwell has sold both his and his wife's for the sake of an organ. As Birdwell and his wife sit in their parlor with the ministry and oversight board, Jess feels they weight of what is to happen. And West writes: before his lips moved his heart began to pray, "lord, deliver thy servant from the snare of his own iniquity.

As the music begins, Jess is on his feet saying, "Friends let us lift our hearts in prayer."

And he prays in a voice that shook the studding of his home. "he went through the Bible, book by book and sinner by sinner. He prayed in the name of Adam, who had sinned and fallen short of grace, of Moses, who had lost the promised land; of David, who had looked with desire on another man's wife. He prayed in the name of Solomon and his follies, of Abraham and his jealousies, and of Jephthah, who kept his word in cruelty; he made music of his own out of his contrition...He left the old testament and prayed for them all, sinners alike in the name of Paul, who what he would not, he did; and of Peter, who said he knew the man not, and of Thomas, who doubted and Judas who betrayed and of that Mary who repented."[34]

His voice rises and falls with the music. It swells with the crescendos and diminishes on the decrescendos. And he does not finish until the last chords of the organ have been played. And then he sits.

---

[34] Jessamyn West. *Music on The Muscatatuck* in *Faith Stories*, C. Michael Curtis, ed. (Houghton-Mifflin: New York, 2003) p 277

Soon the chair of the ministry and oversight committee stands. "Friend, thee's been an instrument of the Lord this night," he said. "Thee's risen to the throne of grace and carried us all upwards on thy pinions. Thy prayer carried us so near to heaven's gates that now and again I thought I could hear angels' voices choiring and the sound of heavenly harps."

And then the ministry and oversight board left with amens whispering and lingering on their tongues.

"We, in every act of life, and through our singing, as long as we are here, are messengers sent for each other: to heal each other, ourselves, and to light the way – to light the way, through our song – to light the way for everyone."

It would be so easy – so very easy – on a day like today to think first of the ways that Jane and her ministry have fed this congregation. I speak as one with authority on this matter – we have doubtless been fed a feast fit for royalty of music and liturgy – and it would be so tempting to think of the function of worship as to feed ourselves or even to light our own way.

But it's not. Pardon me for slightly dated language – but I know there are folks here who know the answer to this question, "What is the chief end of Man?"

The answer is, "To Glorify God and enjoy him forever."

When we worship – I told my own congregation this recently, it is not for ourselves – we are not the audience of worship. We worship for God. We worship because God is worth it.

Our acts of worship look a little different in that light. Indeed, our acts of vocation look a little different in that light – but there is a side effect to worship and it is this – it is as sure a place as I can think of to look for that proverbial mustard seed to take root.

But a caution about that: Pliny the Elder notes in his <u>Natural History</u>, "mustard… is extremely beneficial for the health. It grows entirely wild, though it is improved by being transplanted: but on the other hand, when it has once been sown it is scarcely possible to get the place free of it, as the seed when it falls germinates at once."[35]

---

[35] Pliny the Elder, *Natural History*, translated by Harris Rackham, Loeb, 1950, Book XIX, Chapter LIV

In other words, beware of mustard seed – there might be some side effects to worship.

I love the way Anne Lamott describes the moment when she stumbled into St. Andrew's Presbyterian Church, so hung-over she could be barely stand. She writes, "The last song was so deep and raw and pure that I could not escape. It was as if the people were singing in between the notes, weeping and joyful at the same time, and I felt like their voices or something was rocking me in its bosom, holding me like a scared kid, and I opened up to that feeling – and it washed over me."[36]

Once it gets a root, mustard is hard to eradicate. There is no telling when it will crop up. There is no predicting, when, like God's grace, unbidden it will break into your world and crack you open. That's why Annie Dillard so famously noted that if we knew what we were doing in worship, we'd wear crash helmets. That too, I expect, is why Jane wouldn't let me turn this sermon in an elegiac direction. She has known something very profound all these years, something preachers and musicians struggle to remember and it is this: when we come to worship, we have a tiger by the tail. There is no telling what God is going to do. There is no telling when the mustard seed will bloom into whatever sacred, carefully planned and contrived activities we may have planned. She has known all these years that God doesn't follow predictable patterns and the fastest way to get swept off your feet with the unyielding power of the holy spirit is to think that that we, the body gathered to worship, somehow control the untamable power of God that is unleashed in this time and place. It's not predictable, it's not containable, it's not controllable – like a conflagration that threatens to sweep through the dry brush of tired expectations, the mustard seed will flower when it is ready – it breaks in with God's good grace.

One last thing about Mrs. Leete: about thirty years later I was in the Presbyterian Hospital downtown visiting a member of this congregation, when the chaplain, a mutual friend, said to me, "You should stop by the Emergency Room, Baron. They've brought in Ralph Leete, and it doesn't look good. Frances is down there with him." So I went down there, and Mrs. Leete looked up at me and said, "Do you remember that time you sang *All Creatures of Our God and King* for me?"

It was, and remains for me, an experience of the Kingdom of God.

---

[36] Anne Lamott. *Traveling Mercies*. (Anchor: New York, 1999) p 50

The kingdom of God is like a mustard seed – the smallest of all, and yet it grows into a mighty tree and the birds of the air take their rest in it.

In the name of the Father, and of the Son, and of the Holy Spirit, Amen.

When We Don't Enter the Promised Land
Deuteronomy 34:1-12; 1 Thessalonians 2:1-8

Can I tell you about John Knox? Maybe you've heard of him. We don't know much about his early life… his father was a farmer in Scotland, his mother died when he was a little boy, we're not even sure about his birthday – it's sometime between 1505 and 1515. His father wanted more for him than farming, so he studied at the University of Saint Andrews, where he became a priest and a notary.

Sometime around then, he became persuaded of the rightness of the protestant reformation that was beginning to emerge in Scotland and since we're just covering highlights, I'll come straight to the point: he got caught up in the events that led to the murder of Cardinal David Beaton and when the French Queen Regent of Scotland brought in her friends to help, he was taken prisoner by the French.

He spent two years as a galley slave, rowing in the depths of a boat.

After he was released from slavery, he was exiled to England.

In England, he was charged to the parish of Berwick-upon-Tweed, where he ministered until Mary Tudor became queen of England. Once more he was exiled, this time to Geneva, where he encountered John Calvin, from whom he learned the principles of reformed theology.

He returned to Scotland.

He was exiled back to Geneva.

He returned to Scotland – you should see a trend emerging here – on his last return to Scotland, he was delayed a bit because he couldn't get a visa to pass through England. He'd written a pamphlet entitled, "The First Blast of the Trumpet Against the Monstrous Regiment of Women," and Queen Elizabeth was not amused by it.

He served his last call at St. Giles in Edinburgh, and he died one day after preaching the induction of his successor to that pulpit. The throne of Scotland was still occupied by a woman with whom he vehemently disagreed. The future of the Presbyterian Church in Scotland was by no means yet clear. By no means could it be said that his life's work had been achieved. There is no monument to him other than a stone in the pavement behind the church where it notes that he lies buried somewhere in that parking lot.

John Knox was a man who knew what it was to be disappointed. He was a man who knew what it was to struggle toward an end and yet not to see it achieved.

I love the sense of satisfaction that comes from a goal achieved.

I love the closure that comes with knowing that a task has been completed.

Perhaps you do too… there is something deeply satisfying in meaningful work.

The bigger the task, the more lofty the goal generally, the more satisfying the conclusion of it.

That is why, for me, there are few verses of scripture as poignant as those when Moses is carried by God up to Mount Nebo and shown the Promised Land, because he will not be permitted to enter it.

God was clear early on that Moses would not be allowed to go into the promised land – there are numerous occasions when the reason is given – frankly, the reason ultimately is a moving target. There is something unfair about it – almost unkind even – so much so that Old Testament scholar Patrick Miller equates the denial of Moses's desire to go into the promised land to the disappointment that permeates the book of Job. He writes, "Whether or not Moses is viewed as a tragic figure, certainly the tradition seems to see in his death the unfulfillment of the highest order, in that a life is cut short of the goal toward which it as always been directed. Such failure is often what seems to make death a tragic part of human existence."[37]

There is something so sad about the story of Moses!

I mean, he didn't want the job in the first place – God coerced him at the burning bush way back in Exodus. God made him lead the frequently fickle Israelites – you remember the story a couple of weeks back when God utterly despaired of the Israelites – in an almost comic interlude, God refers to them

---

[37] Patrick Miller. *Deuteronomy*, in *Interpretation*. (John Knox Press: Louisville, 1990) p 243

as Moses's people, to which Moses rather tartly reminds God that they are, in fact, God's people.

It was Moses who listened to the complaints of the Israelites in the wilderness first that they would starve, then that they would die of thirst, then that they didn't have meat, then that their diet was too bland – to the point that God ultimately tells Moses that if they don't shut up, God is going to send so much meat that the Israelites are going to have quail coming out their noses.

This is a tempestuous, roller-coaster of a relationship between God and Moses – and repeatedly, Moses begs to be allowed to go into the land. But, God has decided on a different course. Things will go a different way. Moses will not enter the Promised Land.

It seems resoundingly unfair. It seems resoundingly disappointing.

It's not too much of an overreach to say that the story of Moses has something to say to everyone who ever experienced disappointment.

There's something in this story for everyone who ever worked arduously and long toward an outcome that they will not see realized.

It seems almost cruel on a beautiful Sunday morning to call attention to the fact that we will all face disappointment in our lives. Happy Commitment Season.

But it's true. We do.

Things don't always work out the way we want them to.

Sometimes we work diligently and hard, and still, despite our best efforts, things don't work out.

I don't really want to belabor the point, but if you've ever lived through that time of deep disappointment, you what it is. I don't have to list off things like divorce, downsizing, death and disease for you immediately to know the disappointments of which I'm speaking.

I almost feel bad for bringing it up, except it is almost a universal part of what it means to live this life. We face disappointments.

We don't enter the Promised Land.

I imagine the Promised Land might look a little different for each of us – we are, after all, individuals with various hopes and dreams – and various values. What might seem like a silly disappointment to me might seem monumental to you. Or what seems insignificant to you might been insurmountable to another. What peeves you might pain me.

We are endlessly complex creatures as varied and different as snowflakes and yet the common experience of living this life is that into each of our lives, a little rain will fall.

Or a lot.

Or a devastating flood of hurt.

Interestingly, the author of Deuteronomy never tells us how Moses felt about the Promised Land. God takes Moses up to Mount Nebo and shows him that the promise will be fulfilled and then Moses dies.

It's really not the most hopeful passage of scripture. In fact, I could almost feel bad about preaching on it on a Sunday when we are baptizing beautiful children into the family of God.

Almost.

But there's this little technicality that in turn offers this story a bit of hope: No, Moses will not go to the Promised land, but God does carry Moses to the top of the mountain to see the land.

With that, we know that it's not that God didn't care, but rather that the course of action will be different. Indeed, within the relationship between God and Moses, there is a deep care implied on the part of God. Moses is not just a tool that God decided to use, but rather a mortal with whom God enjoyed a deep and personal relationship. When Moses comes to the end, God does not step back and just let Moses go, but rather carries him to the top of the Mountain and shows him the Promised Land.

And that puts a little different spin this story.

It is to the point of a platitude to say that being God's people doesn't mean that we don't encounter any unpleasantness. We all know that. If we didn't, then every minor head cold would be a constant threat to faith. A hangnail would upend our spiritual lives. It's no secret that Christian faith guarantees us virtually nothing when it comes to living this life.

No, God guarantees us almost nothing, almost nothing.

God guarantees us nothing but God.

That is the promise of baptism – that God is in this thing with us.

And God gave us each other to live that promise out.

Last Wednesday, I came up to the sanctuary with two of the children we will baptize in a few minutes, Eva and Harper, and I wanted them to understand what exactly we would be doing today, and so I tried to explain baptism to them. I explained that they will stand by the font and tell me their names, and that I would touch my wet hand to their heads three times and then I tried to explain what baptism means.

Now, we know theologically, what it means. Baptism is a visible sign of God's invisible grace. We know that it is the sacrament of inclusion – that in baptism, God grafts us onto the body of Christ. But I couldn't quite come up with the right words that could explain that to these children, because, you know being grafted onto the body of Christ is really rather esoteric.

So I just said that you all would make them a promise to always be there for them.

That really is the point of Christian faith – that whatever the challenges, whatever mess we find ourselves in – and we do find ourselves in messes from time to time – that we are all in this mess together, and that God is in this mess with us.

God is always with us. Sometimes in the Promised Land, and sometimes on the mountaintop looking off into an uncertain future. God is always with us.

Since I started with one reformer, I'll end with another. You know it really was a terrifying thing to be a reformer of the church – to take all of the authority of the church – and to say, "No, I just don't really think so."

It takes a special kind of conviction to be excommunicated.

It takes a special kind of commitment to row in the galley of a slave ship for two years like Knox.

It takes a special kind of conviction to nail ninety-five complaints to a door and go into hiding like Martin Luther.

It's hard to wander through the wilderness and not know whether you will ever reach the Promised Land.

A story is told of Luther – he suffered terribly from melancholy. Today we'd have treatment for the kind of anxiety and fear with which he lived. Peter Hobbie reminded us last weekend that once, when Luther's friends saw him in a period of terrible despondency, they noticed he was writing something, over and over again. When he got up and walked away, they went and looked at what he had written.

Over and over, he had written one word, *baptismo.*

Time and again, Luther comforted himself with the assurance, "You are baptized."

That was his comfort. That was his assurance: that he rested always, as you do, and as I do, in God's care.

When the pope's emissary threatened him with excommunication, he challenged Luther, "And when you have been abandoned by the princes, and when you have been deserted by the people, where, brother Martin, where will you be then?" "Then as now," answered Luther, "in the hands of Almighty God."

In the name of the Father, and of the Son, and of the Holy Ghost, Amen.

When the Heavens Open
Isaiah 64:1-9; Mark 13:24-37

You have this life. God has given it to you with the expectation that it will have meaning and purpose and it is moving along. You are the steward of this life. No one else can do that for you.

This past week, I read two stories in the news about lives being lived incredibly well – not in the high on the hog sense, but just with incredible value and humanity.

Maurice Rowland and Miguel Alvarez were members of the staff of Valley Springs Manor. Maurice was a cook and Miguel was a janitor.

But their roles changed abruptly when the facility where they worked shut down without taking care of the residents who lived there.

For three days, until the Fire and Police departments were able to take over, they were left with 16 residents of the assisted living center when the staff stopped getting paid and most left. But Maurice and Miguel had a conversation in the kitchen about caring for the residents, some of whom suffered from dementia.

Alvarez said, "If we would have left, they wouldn't have nobody."

Rowland said, "I just couldn't see myself going home – next thing you know, they're in the kitchen trying to cook their own food and burn the place down," he said. "Even though they weren't our family, they were kind of like our family for this short period of time."[38]

There are turning points in each of our lives where we are offered choices. How we decide leaves an indelible mark on our very selves. The last line of the StoryCorps broadcast of Maurice and Miguel was, "If I would have left, I would have had that on my conscience for a long time."

The things that we do sort of get into us, don't they?

---

[38] *NPR News*, November 21, 2014

I don't know whether Rowland and Alvarez spent much time in the moment thinking of the consequence of their decisions – just that they did what they did because they knew they needed to.

There are surely times of consequence in each of our lives, aren't there?

It may seem odd to think of these things when the scriptures today seem so apocalyptic. I know most of us probably avoid those sections of the Bible, but they have a point. They are there for a reason…

When you read the apocalyptic parts of the Bible, do your eyes glaze over? Or do they pique your curiosity?

The history of interpretation of scripture is littered with incorrect doomsday predictions. I used to get particularly tickled by attempting to come up with the most nonsensical versions possible in order to utterly discredit that particular (wrong) way of reading Scripture, and there are some doozies to be sure, but I wonder if we take these passages seriously enough?

They have a history of course.

Some whole books of the Bible are apocalyptic, of course, like the book of Revelation, but mostly there are just passages that are slipped in amongst other passages of the Bible. They occur in the Old Testament (such as what we read from Isaiah) as well as the new, such as what we read from Mark, and for the most part they stick out like a sore thumb. They seem to make no earthly sense whatsoever.

You'll be reading along through Mark's Gospel, for instance, and in the middle of parables and miracles and healings, there will crop of a strange series of verses where it appears that Jesus has been transported to almost another dimension. He starts talking about things like the heavens being opened, or the stars falling from the sky, or mountains quaking. Generally, there are clouds involved, sometimes trumpets, and angels are hovering somewhere nearby.

It's fantastical and it's supposed to be. It's certainly not meant to be taken literally – bad theology abounds when it is taken literally, and the ancients would never have done so. They knew it was intended to be evocative.

It's supposed to evoke, not educate on future activities.

What it is supposed to *evoke* in us is a feeling that something more is happening than we can see in the present tense.

It can't quite be decoded. There's no par for par equivalency between actions or characters in apocalyptic and real-life. The Roman emperor might be the beast in one selection and a dragon in another. There are a few other choice turns of phrase that describe that particular individual, but the point is we're supposed to hear them and know that whatever present circumstances might look like, that what we're looking at now isn't the whole story.

The whole story is always the story of the unfolding urgency of God's grace and God's redemptive power at a foundational level and for those under bad circumstances. These fantastical renderings of what God is going to do are a marker that, no matter what happens, God remains the bedrock on which all of creation rests and in God's redemptive judgment, injustices will not be allowed to stand.

Apocalyptic is language for oppressed communities, and I wonder sometimes if it has much to say to those of us who aren't feeling all that oppressed.

Because whenever privileged people start talking about oppression, we need to be sure of two things: First, that we don't confuse ourselves for the oppressed. There are a lot of different ways to be treated badly. That's not the same as oppression. Second, we need to be certain that we don't substitute our own understanding of what it means to be held down and marginalized for that of those who actually are.

Because if we don't learn and know what is really going on, then pretty much anything we have to say on matters of oppression is going to miss the mark. My friend Regina Langley tells me that it is only when we understand what we *don't* understand that we can have an honest conversation about oppression.

When the language of oppression is used by the privileged to refer to garden variety annoyances, it is almost proof-positive that it is resting on a foundation of cheap, trite grace.

You know what I mean by that. It's grace without consequence.

It's grace without impact.

Under no circumstances should we maintain a trite understanding of grace.

Because surely our lives are of consequence, aren't they?

Perhaps you've read the novella, <u>The Picture of Dorian Gray</u>. It's a marvelous little book by Oscar Wilde, one of the great wits of history. The premise of the book is simple. Dorian Gray has an enchanted portrait – it is painted when he was a young man – and the enchantment is that he can do anything he wants in his life – and the effects will only show on the portrait. He can live an utterly debauched life and he will pay no physical consequence for it – but the portrait will show absolutely everything.

Which, of course, Gray does, and the picture becomes hideously deformed and monstrous as his misdeeds of excessive living – alcoholism and opium consumption, sexual relations treated casually while the other thought they were serious commitments – the misdeeds pile up and the portrait grows ever more grotesque.

Wilde's point is that what we do marks us at a deep level – much deeper than the skin.

Our lives are of consequence, and so God's grace cannot be inconsequential.

The apocalyptic passages of the Bible are small in-breakings of the assurance that God will, in the final estimation, *not* allow grace to be inconsequential.

I know that these apocalyptic passages sometimes appear to be so wrathful.

Do you know what God's wrath is? It's God's love denied.

God is good, and God is love, and God's love always wins. Wrath is the mechanism by which God's love ultimately prevails, because make no mistake about it, God's love *always* prevails.

These apocalyptic road-markers are reminders that no matter what we think is going on – all of creation – the whole shebang, the universe and everything inside and outside it, are resting on the bedrock of God and God has certain values that do not change.

Grace is the in-breaking of *God's* reality into *present* reality with the assurance that God will settle for nothing less than what is good.

That is why grace is so significant. It's never cheap or trite, except perhaps in our own minds.

I watched a marvelous movie last week, *Quartet*.

It features the magnificent Maggie Smith and Billy Connolly, and it is set in the Beecham House Home for Retired Musicians. It was where opera singers and musicians would go to retire and live out their days. It centers on two characters, Reggie and Jean, who were briefly married and whose pinnacle of their respective careers was a particular quartet from Rigoletto for which Reggie received nine curtain calls and Jean, twelve.

And after that their lives spectacularly fell apart in ways that are never fully expressed – only that Jean, under the effects of too much champagne, indulged a fling that destroyed the marriage.

Fate brings them back together in their dotage at Beecham House. When Jean and Reggie confront one another, she recites a rehearsed speech.

Reggie storms off.

Jean follows him until she corners him in a church.

Then she repeats her rehearsed speech.

Back and forth they go – bitterness meets contrition. Pride meets love. Vanity makes a few appearances.

How do often bitterness, pride and vanity stand in the way of grace?

It is only after time that healing can enter in. Of course, in the end, they sing the quartet.

God's goodness is never contained in rehearsed prayers or prepared speeches. Always God's grace emerges at the intersection of honesty and humanity.

When I say that there are times of consequence, I do not mean there are times when you will be made to pay. I mean there are times when clarity dispels the possibility of self-deception and you know how things are and you know what must be done.

Apologies to our opera singers, but I can't resist the analogy: apocalyptic is the opera of the Bible. It's grand. It's bold. It's meant to make a statement.

And that statement is the reassurance to the oppressed community that God's love is still the bedrock on which all of creation rests.

And that statement is also the reassurance to the privileged community that God's love will permit no convenient self-deceptions.

Our lives are precious gifts and they are moving along, and there is nothing without consequence, good or bad, in the final estimation.

Apocalyptic is vivid (like opera) and so I expect the images of sin and grace that this sermon evokes are vivid as well.

But goodness and justice are frequently lived out in less apocalyptic ways.

So, the other story I heard this week came from the BBC.

Ruby Holt, 101 years old, had never seen the ocean.

Mark Davis, executive director of Brookdale's Sterling House in Tennessee, where Ms. Holt lives, said two employees filled out the application for her after finding out that she wanted to see the ocean for the first time. It turns out that two of the employees were having a water-gun fight one day and that lead to the topic of water, which lead to the subject of the beach and then Ms. Holt, who has four children, said she was always too busy on the farm or working in a shirt factory to travel and that the family never had enough money.

The holiday to the beach in Alabama was the furthest she had ever been from her home in Giles County. Ms. Holt said she had only left the state of Tennessee once before.

"When we got to the room yesterday she was just pointing out the ocean and, you know, her facial expressions and... she was just speechless."[39]

No, decidedly, all of life is not apocalyptic. Sometimes it's rather simple. But it is always of consequence.

You have this life. God has given it to you with the expectation of meaning and purpose, and it is moving along. You are the steward of your life. No one else can do it for you.

In the name of the Father, and of the Son, and of the Holy Ghost, Amen.

---

[39] *BBC News*, 21 November 2014

Part Four:

Love: Variations on A Theme

Love
1 Corinthians 13

Let's get one thing quite clear: this is not a sweet passage. I don't do syrupy or saccharine very well and thought of preaching a sermon on a saccharine, syrupy selection of scripture is about more than I can tolerate. I would imagine the only thing much worse than preaching it would be listening to it.

Archbishop Desmond Tutu, the retired Archbishop of Cape Town in South Africa and the head of the Truth and Reconciliation commission, has a wonderful book. It is entitled, <u>God Has a Dream, A Vision of Hope for Our Time</u>.

Tutu begins each chapter with the words, *dear child of God.* With these words, he sets the tone of what is to follow, affirmation of the worth of human life, of the infinite value that God places on each of us. The titles of two of the central chapters are: *God loves you as you are,* and *God loves your enemies.* Tutu writes:

"Dear child of God, in our world it is often hard to remember that God loves you just as you are. God loves you not because you are good, no, God loves you, period. God loves us not because we are lovable. No, we are lovable precisely because God loves us. It is marvelous when you come to understand that you are accepted for who you are, apart from any achievement."[40]

Likewise, he continues in the next chapter:

"Dear child of God, if we are truly to understand that God loves all of us, we must recognize that he loves our enemies, too. God does not share our hatred, no matter what the offence we have endured. We try to claim God for ourselves and our cause, but God's love is too great to be confined to any one side of a conflict or any one religion. And our prejudices, regardless of whether they are based on religion, race, nationality, gender, sexual orientation, or anything else, are absolutely and utterly ridiculous in God's eyes."[41]

Which perhaps leaves us with question, what does it mean to love the way God loves?

---

[40] Desmond Tutu. *God Has a Dream: A Vision of Hope for Our Time.* pp 31-32
[41] Ibid, pp 43-44

About the first thing we have to do regarding this scripture we have read this morning is peel away any romantic preconceptions we have attached to it. As previously stated, this is not a sweet scripture. It is not a scripture intended for dewy eyed brides and grooms to swoon over on their wedding day. I am so often asked to read this passage for weddings and reflect on it that I have been honing a wedding homily about this passage for years now, and among the points I regularly make about it is that it is not about romance and wedding day good feelings. No, to fairly and rightly consider this scripture we have to step away from all of the drivel that Hollywood has pedaled about what love is and is not and consider that Paul presents a competing vision about what *God* says about love. To be sure, the Bible does have things to say about romantic love, and there can be application of this text for our romantic lives if we are so inclined, but this isn't a passage about romance.

The ancient city of Corinth enjoyed a reputation somewhat akin to Vegas. Some say Corinth had gone respectable by the time of the establishment of the church, but one of the assumptions that we can make given this context is that the church represented at least something of a countercultural voice in the city. Second, Paul seems to think that as a countercultural voice, this church he has founded leaves a little something to be desired. On occasion, it seems the Christians in Corinth had missed some pretty significant opportunities to demonstrate that God's way is different than the other ways. Third, these missed opportunities, painfully, were directly in the church. The First Pauline Church of Corinth had experienced some growing pains. It was also a congregation that contained some Christians who experienced some personal growing pains as they sought, albeit not as robustly as Paul would like, to learn how to be Christian. Paul wrote to them out of concern for their well-being as a congregation. He wanted them to know what love looks like.

Personal application of this text, though, may be a bit of a challenge. If you do not love someone, it is rather hard to manufacture feelings. You might be able to grow to love someone – after all, years and years of arranged marriages have demonstrated just that – but again, this is not a passage about romantic love. This is a passage about the love that God calls us to demonstrate – in the church and in ourselves – in order that we might be a valid witness to who God is and what God is about.

Essentially, this passage makes three points – first, that religious practice not rooted in love is largely irrelevant. Second, that love has some distinctive characteristics. Finally, whatever spiritual gifts we may possess, in the end, it is love that abides and endures. Love is serious. The calling to love is serious. If love is not to be disingenuous, we cannot let it be only about romanticism and sentimentality, there must be some *substance* to our claims to love.

The challenge Paul faced in writing this letter remains today: personal experiences that we have of love get in the way of hearing what Paul had to say. Our very human experiences of loss, frustration and betrayal as well as faithfulness, endurance, support and nurture combine to give us a view of love that is tempered by an incomplete understanding of the self-giving nature of love. It is the subject of late-night dorm discussions, popular media and even serious discourse whether or not truly self-giving love is possible. At the heart of our experiences, we – I – always remain the center of the experience of love. *I* love this person. *I* want to show this person my devotion. *I* need to demonstrate the love I feel. Love, unexamined, can even be perceived as a selfish emotion.

But love described by Paul is not. Love, described by Paul, is the very expression of Christian vocation.

Of course, love in the abstract is very difficult to comprehend and Paul gives the Corinthians a number of adjectives of what love looks like. Patient, kind, not envious, boastful or rude. Actually, like Jesus.

Yes, actually, the revelation we have of Jesus Christ is about love. I cannot think of another word to describe what God has demonstrated to us.

And as imperfect as our witness and our understanding may be, there are those saints who have shown us love. I think of Dietrich Bonhoeffer, a martyr for Christianity, executed by the Nazis, who wrote: "God himself has undertaken to teach brotherly love; all that men can add to it is to remember this divine instruction and the admonition to excel in it more and more… When God was merciful to us, we learned to be merciful with our brethren. When we received forgiveness instead of judgment, we, too, were made ready to forgive our brethren. What God did to us, we then owed to others. The more we received, the more we were able to give… This God himself taught us to meet one another as God has met us in Christ."[42] There are indeed saints among us who have taught us love.

No, this is not a sweet passage of scripture, but it is an important one. Love is important in our Christian vocation. It is the cornerstone. Without love, we gain nothing.

---

[42] Dietrich Bonhoeffer. *Life Together.* p 24

But the hard part is when we encounter that which does not inspire easy love in us. The hard part is where our experience does not point us in the direction of love, but of hatred sometimes, but more often, indifference.

It's not always easy to love. We are too often struggling to do the best that we can with the junk we're hauling along with us to get it right.

But Jesus showed love. He told stories about what love looks like. Do you remember the one about the fellow who was going down the road and he got mugged and left for dead? Two fine people walk by and did nothing, but then somebody came along and picked him up, put him in his own car and took him to the hospital and said he'd pay the bill. Or maybe you remember a rebellious young man who decided he wanted to get out and live so he asked for an early payout on his inheritance. He wandered off where he shouldn't have gone and did things he shouldn't do with people with whom he shouldn't have done them. He blew it all and decided it was time to come home, and his father, seeing his train-wreck of a child, ran across the fields to greet him in great joy.

To know Jesus is to see what love looks like, to see the love that Paul did his best to describe. In our most Christian moments, we remember what God has done for us and it moves us to similar action.

Love is not weak.

Love does not cause us to sit around staring dreamily into each other's eyes in a sort of mutual admiration society. Love is patient, kind, enduring, bearing, believing – but love is not weak.

Indeed, evangelical pastor Rob Bell got the message down to two words which he used to title his book about salvation: *Love Wins*.

What Paul is admonishing the Corinthian Christians to do, to remember and live, is that love is at its very heart, a call to action, a different kind of action, a Christ-like kind of action. It is a different thing to love the way that Jesus loves.

When Jesus was asked what was the most important commandment, he replied with a very succinct old creed of Judaism: love the Lord your God with all your heart, soul, mind and strength, and love your neighbor as yourself.

This is what love looks like: Love is patient, love is kind, love is not envious or boastful or arrogant or rude. It does not insist on its own way; it is not irritable or resentful; it does not rejoice in wrongdoings, but rejoices in the truth. It bears all things, believes all things, hopes all things, endures all things.

Love can be a slippery concept. It is hard to quantify – Paul didn't even manage to quantify it. He could only describe it, and his description is incomplete. It's a good description, but there is more to love than just what Paul recited.

Archbishop Tutu rewrote his book a few years later to be appropriate for children. He wrote, "Each of us carries a piece of God's heart within is. And when we love one another, the pieces of God's heart are made whole.

That's what love does. It makes everything whole. Love makes a new creation.

It reminds me of my favorite hymn, "How Can I Keep from Singing?" I love all the verses, but it is the refrain that I love most. Some versions sing, "Since Christ is Lord of heaven and earth…" but Robert Lowry's original words sang, "Since Love is Lord of Heaven and earth, how can I keep from singing?"

And so it is. Love is Lord of heaven and earth – how can we keep from singing?

In the name of the Father, and of the Son, and of the Holy Ghost, Amen.

A Love-Song Gone Wrong
Isaiah 5:1-7; Luke 12:49-56

There are some experiences in life that serve as timely notices that one should not follow a given career path. When I interned as a hospital chaplain many years ago, it was a resounding clarion that I was not being called to this manner of service. I worked in the Cancer Center and Harris Hospice Unit at Presbyterian Hospital in Charlotte. It wasn't that I was so bad at it, though I have shared some of my less stellar moments with you; it was that the work utterly and completely exhausted me, and that is a sign one that is usually worth paying attention to.

So, one Friday afternoon, after three of the patients I was attending to died on the same day, including a young child, an old friend of mine called and said, "How about going to see *Saving Private Ryan*?"

"Absolutely not. A million times no," I replied, "But I could be talked into going to see *There's Something about Mary*."

Now, before you go home and find this on Netflix, I need to say that it was exactly what the doctor ordered because the humor was, at times, exquisite in its crudeness.

It's not a typical romantic comedy in that Mary, a surgeon, has fled her old life with her special needs brother, shedding most markers of her identity, to escape an obsessive old flame. Ben Stiller's character hires a private eye to track her down, and hilarity ensues.

Though Mary ends up with the least psychotic man in love with her in the end, it is not the stuff of which sonnets are written. It is decidedly a love song gone wrong, hence the humor.

Spurned love isn't always humorous though.

When I was living in Scotland one summer, there was a BBC program, in case you think the BBC only produces highbrow material, highlighting the reaction of a series of cuckolded spouses. The program featured an interview with Lady Sarah Graham Moon, who is best known for her spectacularly coordinated retaliation to her husband's infidelity, pouring white paint on her cheating husband's BMW, distributing his life-time accumulated collection of vintage claret to friends and neighbors, and most notably, for her treatment of his extensive wardrobe of Savile Row suits. Well, the Beeb interviewed

Lady Sarah about this particular aspect of her revenge and in the interview, she recounts the feeling of sitting in the floor of his closet with scissors and his favorite suit, having shredded it, and she said, "As I was holding up the remnants of the suit and shears, I thought to myself, 'This is madness. It will take me hours to do all of these suits." So she cut the bottom six inches off of every sleeve in the closet, leaving them in a pile for the philandering lord to find.

There is something about rejected and demeaned love that cuts to the heart of the lover.

It is the experience of rejected and demeaned love that prompts the somewhat dystopic love-song from Isaiah that we read today.

Generally, love songs are sung by one of the lovers, but in this instance, it is the prophet who is singing about the love that God has for the vineyard, and it is a love that seems decidedly pointless.

It's almost a ballad, as the prophet says, "Let me tell you about my beloved..." And so, Isaiah sings of the effort and cultivation that God has poured into this vineyard, placing it in the choicest location, planting it with the best of seeds, preparing the winepress and setting up the watchtower.

It is a vineyard that is expected to yield good things.

But then the song turns. The key changes. Christopher Seitz writes, "The song turns into a prophetic indictment. The singer invites his listeners to hear about the careful attention his friend showered on the vineyard and of the disappointment he experienced when the vineyard yielded nothing but rank grapes... Moreover, the 'song' format elicits the more gossipy side of their interest; everyone has a perverse interest in love gone wrong."[43]

Then the song shifts again, and the singer has been swept aside as well; it is God, now, who sings of heart-broken disappointment.

God sings of a frenzy of activity: What has gone wrong? Did God not do enough? Are the grapes the wrong kind? The questions come in staccato succession, each leaving the listener little opportunity to render an opinion.

---

[43] Christopher Seitz, *Isaiah* in *Interpretation*. (John Knox Press: Louisville, 1993) p 47

No sooner do the questions end than the judgment is given: the vineyard will be torn down. The hedges will be ripped up. No longer will God hoe and water it.

The vineyard is the people Israel, and the verdict is rendered.

Just what sort of God are we talking about there?

This love seems to be a perverse sort of love, one that turns in jealous rage to anger.

In the New York Times this week, Amy Shumer reviewed some of her favorite books, and she came to a play. She wrote about the play "Who's Afraid of Virginia Woolf?"

"When I was in my 20s, I thought the yelling and drinking and sexy anger between Elizabeth Taylor and Richard Burton was what love was supposed to look like. The endless brown liquor drinks, the cigarettes always being freshly lit in Elizabeth Taylor's very lipsticked mouth, and the unbridled, constant rage. It was all so appealing to me. By the way, that movie has a knockout dance scene as well, when Elizabeth Taylor dances with George Segal's character while simultaneously screaming at her husband on the sidelines.[44]"

So there is God, acting to any casual observer, like an unhinged lover.

What is going on here?

To answer that question, we need to address what God is *not* before we seek to understand any of the attributes or actions of God that can be affirmed.

God is not: a fairy godmother, a capricious cop, or a vending machine.

Quickly, God is not a fairy godmother. We are not Cinderella staying home from the ball to clean the scullery and God isn't going to show up to turn pumpkins into a coach or mice into horses. No kidding. God doesn't exist to make us happy. God cares about us, but God does not exist to make us happy.

---

[44] A version of this article appears in print on August 14, 2016, on page BR8 of the Sunday Book Review with the headline: Amy Schumer

Nor is God a capricious cop. God isn't following us around to invent new rules to pull us over and rattle our brains with criminal code. God doesn't exist to keep score of our performance.

And God is most certainly not a vending machine. Our tithes and offerings get us nothing from God. They enable Christian community and ministry to continue in the manner we believe God wants us to go, but there is no quid-pro-quo with God. Prayers are the same way. Mark Twain noted this in *Huckleberry Finn* when Huck put a box under the bed and prayed it be filled with gold and concluded the next day that prayer didn't work when no gold appeared.

There are many things the flights of our imagination may suggest about God, and God exceeds any imagination, but there is no give and take here. We are not equals.

What God is, then, is *good.*

And goodness, when we are talking about God, is not a negotiable scale. There are not gradations of goodness. Something is not "kind of" good. It's all or nothing. Something is good or it is not.

Think of the days of creation: God made things, and because they were made by good, they were good, and God called them thusly.

But this vineyard, it is not good. God made it, but it has been corrupted. It cannot remain God's vineyard while it is corrupted.

And God is *love.*

What a freighted word *love* is!

We twist its meaning by reducing it to the function of eroticism or gut it to meaninglessness by making its brotherly or sisterly nature contractual rather than relational. But however we load love up like a boxcar with all of our sinfully incomplete and corrupted viewpoints, it is still God who defines *love* by God's being.

And it is the overflowing of God's being, the overflowing of God's love, where God makes creation and places us in it.

I could go on but I don't want to risk confusing the point by belaboring it, and it is this:

God's good love is not interchangeable with any substitute.

If God seems jealous in the pages of the Bible, it is because God won't accept lesser substitutes for the birthright of loving relationship that God granted to humankind in breathing God's own breath into us.

So the corrupted vineyard has to go and the tainted people must be called back to goodness.

So the cuckolded lover remains, not vindictive, but instead working for redemption.

Indeed, when we read from the pages of the Gospel such words as we heard from Jesus this morning, it can be easy to gloss over them and put them quickly away from us – who, after all, wants to dwell on the moments when Jesus suggests that the Christian way will bring division?

Nobody enjoys division and separation, not healthy people at least.

Sure, some may revel in regressive tribalism where the world can be divided into winners and losers, haves and have-nots, clean and unclean, holy and profane. There are always those who like clear and plain boundaries between us and them, or between me and thee.

There are always those who want to divide the world up, but healthy people shy away from using conflict to create dividing walls, and here is Jesus, speaking in rather graphic terms of what his message will bring.

Do you know what Jesus is saying at the heart of it all?

He's saying that bad can't be good, and it's pointless to pretend like it is.

He's saying that hate can't be love, and it's pointless to pretend like it is.

To the casual observer both the vineyard song and Jesus' song of fire sound like love songs gone wrong, but in fact, they are not.

In fact, they are the expression of love that understands what it is to love unconditionally.

Does that seem surprising?

Think of it: conditional love is conditions based.

But God's love is not conditional because if the conditions aren't good, God is going to sweep them away, because God's love is good, and good is not conditional either.

If at this point you are struggling with a question, you are not alone. If the question is, "If God is good, and cannot settle for less than good, and God is love and will not settle for less than love, where do I, *who am not perfect*, fit into this?

The answer, for a Christian, is simple: you fit into this in Jesus Christ. I am not, in this moment, concerned with how other faiths answer this question. For the Christian, God has sung us into this love-song in the person of Jesus Christ.

God cannot settle for less than goodness and love, and so Jesus Christ is God's answer to the brokenness of the world.

And if God answers the love-song-gone-wrong in this way, what is expected from us?

Love.

I could *so* end right now with a tear-jerker love story. I have one, and I'll tell it to you later if you want it, but that's not going to help us right now because love can be esoteric and we need the practical when it comes to making the love-song go right. So here are some practical tips:

> 1) Exercise a zero-tolerance policy toward hate. Whether in speech, print, implication or the lesser impulses of our own minds, cut it out. Don't indulge it. Be the person whose principles your friends have to tolerate.
>
> 2) Pretend to love people. Pretending effectively will require you to act like you love them. Don't worry if you feel fake, do it anyway, they might believe you. The world will be a better place because of it and Saint Paul says it has the added advantage of making your enemies crazy. C.S. Lewis warns that this behavior is catching: acting loving might make you start to feel loving.
>
> 3) Forgive. Golly gee this one is difficult. But here's an inside scoop: forgiving will change you also.

Three is enough to get us started. If you feel like an overachiever, pray for your enemies.

There's plenty enough working against God's goodness and God's love in this world. Be on the right side.

In the name of the Father, and of the Son, and of the Holy Ghost, Amen.

True Love
1 Corinthians 13; Jeremiah 1:4-10

A seminary professor was known for preaching so eloquently on the topic of *love* that he was invited to preach in multiple congregations around the same area. One couple was so touched by the sermon that they approached him after the service was over and asked that he might speak with their nineteen-year-old daughter whom they describe as an "alcoholic and out of control." The professor agreed to meet with her and was able to make an assessment on their first visit. He said, "When I first saw her, I thought, 'Young lady, if you're feeling alright, would you please tell your face.'" She was totally unhappy with a very negative attitude.

The story goes that they met several times, and each time the professor became more convinced that the young woman's problem was that she was completely self-absorbed... indeed, he described her as the most self-centered person he had ever met. Finally, one day, he confronted her with her self-absorption. He said, "You know what you need? You need a Copernican revelation. You need to know the world doesn't revolve around you. You live in a world whose population is one." The girl stomped out of his office and never came back.

About a month later, the professor met a psychiatrist who had come for a lecture at the seminary, so he quizzed the psychiatrist, "How do you get someone to love, not to be self-centered?"

The psychiatrist asked him why he asked such a question, and the professor told the story of the young woman.

The psychiatrist replied to him, "I don't think you can get people to love. It's a decision of the will and a commitment. People must decide to love and commit themselves to it, or they'll never do it. But if you really wanted to help that young lady to love, if you wanted to help her do that, you went about it the wrong way."

The two went back and forth for a few more minutes.

The psychiatrist asked the professor, "Have you ever had a toothache?"

"Yes," the professor replied.

"And what did you think about," the psychiatrist asked.

"Well, I thought about me."

"And what else?"

"I thought about finding a dentist."

"That's right," the psychiatrist responded. "When you are in pain, you cannot think about other people. You think about your pain and how to find someone to help. And the girl came to you thinking, "Maybe this person can help me, and so she came out from behind the mask and revealed herself to you. And she *is* selfish because she is hurting so much. Someone has given her such a bad image of herself that she reflects that image and it comes out as selfish, uncaring and worthless. She's just playing the role they gave her. And she doesn't come to church, not because she doesn't want to, but because she thinks if she does that God might say to her, 'What are *you* doing here.' And you said you didn't like her either."

"I never said that," replied the professor.

"Oh, you didn't? When you said, 'You need a Copernican revelation. Your world has a population of one.' You didn't have to say, 'I don't like you.'"[45]

Have you ever been tempted to say something like that?

I confess that I have. I was worse than tempted. Recently I wrote one of those seemingly soul-satisfying screeds that we all want to write from time to time. And then I hit *send.*

It felt exhilarating for about ten seconds. Then I realized what I'd done.

Have you ever done that?

I immediately followed up with another note, apologizing to my colleagues and asking them to forgive me for my rather uncharitable characterization of someone who had gotten under my skin.

---

[45] Frank Pollard, *How to Do Love* in *Great Preaching 1999*, Mark Johnson, ed. (Preaching Resources: Jackson TN, 1999) Pp39-40 (edited by author for brevity and clarity)

That is sort of the situation that Paul encountered in the Corinthian church that led him to write the extraordinary hymn to love that we encounter here in the 13th chapter.

Aren't those words just wonderful? Who *wouldn't* want to love like that and to be loved like that? I read this passage a lot at weddings and I think that is because it is so deeply aspirational. We all want to know that this kind of love is possible, even if it's fleeting, and rare.

But too often, we get Copernican revelations and unfortunate e-mails.

It is hard work to commit to love. It is hard work to commit to love when what we encounter seems closer to self-absorption and unkindness than it does to the divine love of Christ.

This is so often true that Frederick Buechner also echoes the sentiment that love is a choice. He writes, "In the Christian sense, love is not primarily an emotion, but an act of the will. When Jesus tells us to love our neighbors, he is not telling us to love them in the sense of responding to them with a cozy emotional feeling. You can as easily produce a cozy emotional feeling on demand as you can yawn or sneeze. On the contrary, he is telling us to love our neighbors in the sense of being willing to work for their well-being even if it means sacrificing our own well-being to that end, even if it means sometimes just leaving them alone. Thus in Jesus' terms, we can love our neighbors without necessarily liking them. In fact, liking them may stand in the way of loving them by making us overprotective sentimentalists instead of reasonably honest friends."[46]

Which is to say that whatever love is, love is primarily a choice.

What is particularly interesting to me is that, in a great hymn to love, Paul takes a moment to identify what love is *not*. He writes,

Love is not envious or boastful or arrogant or rude. It does not insist on its own way; it is not irritable or resentful; it does not rejoice in wrongdoing, but rejoices in the truth.

Now, please note, Paul is not saying that we are not frequently all of these things. We may indeed be envious, boastful, arrogant or rude. We may often insist on our own ways, and be irritable or resentful. Occasionally we may be happy that we got away with wrongdoing. Paul does not claim that these

---

[46] Frederick Buechner, *Wishful Thinking, A Seeker's ABC.* (HarperOne: San Francisco, 1993) p 65

things do not happen. Indeed, he does not claim that Christians do not *do* these things from time to time.

Indeed, for Paul to claim such would have been laughable to the Corinthian Christians. They knew perfectly well that their neighbors could be petty, rude, mean and self-absorbed, and that despite being Christians!

No, Paul is very realistic in his assessment of the Corinthian Church.

And he knew that it was not *love* that motivates such actions.

And so, it is that as I speak to you today about true love, I want to be very clear in not confusing what love is.

Love is none of the things that Paul says it is not. And the church has been guilty on occasion of propping up such behaviors by encouraging our members to live into relationships that tolerate such behaviors to the exclusion of loving one's own self. Let me be very plain: if you are in a relationship that is characterized by abusive behavior, God wants you to have help. God wants the abuse to stop. Sometimes abuse stops because of a change of behavior. Sometimes it stops because of change of relationship. But make no mistake about it: God does not delight in seeing God's creations beaten down. So, if you are in a situation of abuse, please talk to me. Please talk to Drew. Please talk to Sarah Kate if talking to a male is uncomfortable. And I say these things because love is an act of will, and loving oneself is an act of will. And you deserve to be loved.

And when we love and are loved, God is served in the world.

I have been honing a marriage homily for roughly 15 years now, some of you probably have heard it – well, actually, I've preached it at some of your weddings. And if you haven't, it goes something like this: Love gives us the chance to show the world what God is like. Marriage is a vocation because God is glorified when people see what love looks like.

Like I said, I've been honing this homily for fifteen years because I believe it reflects a tiny, miniscule, incomplete and inadequate bit of what God is like.

Elsewhere in the New Testament, we read that *God is love*.

It's so interesting. God didn't have to make creation. God is complete in and unto God's own self. God's creation of humankind didn't come about due to some inadequacy of God's being. Rather, theologians say, God made creation out of the overflowing of God's love.

And it is the overflowing of God's love that will address the pain of the world. Just as the psychiatrist earlier diagnosed the pain of the individual as the root cause of self-centeredness, so the brokenness of sin is the root cause of violation of *shalom* that exhibits itself in so much hurt in the world.

It is the overflowing of love that will heal the world. Indeed, it is *only* the overflowing of love that will heal the world.

That overflowing is ongoing, but it is not yet complete.

For many years, I passed by a weathered bronze plaque on the wall of the McKay center at Princeton Seminary. The McKay center was the refectory of the school, so we passed by it every time we had a meal. The plaque was placed by the class of 1953 in memory of their friend James Joseph Reeb, who was killed in the marches of Selma, Alabama. He responded to a call from Dr. King to come, and to march, and on the night of March 9th, fell to the sidewalk after a crushing blow to the skull. His classmates placed the marker in memorial to him. Years later, the seminary invited a member of the class of 1953 to preach in chapel to commemorate the Selma march. His classmate wanted to appeal to those gathered to work for the healing of the world, and he began by listing the ways he might appeal to those listening. He might appeal by long friendship. Or he might appeal to them by citing great social concern. He might appeal to them on the basis of Princeton's tradition of leadership, he said. But then he said, "None of these is adequate. I can appeal to you only on one basis: that we join together in coming to grips with this question: 'What am I, as a Christian, to do?' Not what am I as an individual, or as a citizen, or even as a member of this seminary community, but "What am I, *as a Christian*, to do?"" [47]

That is the heart of Paul's hymn to love in 1 Corinthians. Love is an act of the will. And to love is to be joined to God's ongoing work of reconciling the whole of creation. It is to be invited to bear all things, believe all things, hope all things, endure all things.

Love, as I have said, is a vocation. Love is a holy calling. Love is born out in marriage as well as in friendship, sometimes at the same time. Love is lived in church and in the home. If there is any hope for redemption of the world,

---

[47] Richard J. Oman. *No Greater Love* in *The Princeton Seminary Bulletin.* Series 2, 1995. p 224

it is in that God first loved us, indeed, that the great redemption epic of Christian faith is God's love letter to the world.

A story is told of a little boy whose sister was suffering from a rare blood disorder. It was determined that a transfusion was needed, and knowing that the best hope for recovery would come from a transfusion from her brother, he was asked by the nurse if he could be very brave and give her his blood.

The boy bit his lip and said, "No."

They pleaded with him, and finally he relented. They placed the needle, and only after he began giving blood did he begin to cry. Worried that he was in pain, they rushed to him.

"Does it hurt," they asked?

"No," he managed to get out through his sobs.

"Well, what is it," they asked him.

Finally, he managed to ask the question that troubled him, "How long will it take for me to die?"

It was only then that they realized that he didn't understand that they only needed a pint of his blood.

That is the love of God, love sees the self-centeredness of the world and knows that it is but a symptom of deep hurt. That is the love of God, that gives of itself the point of depletion, to the point of death, even death on a cross.

Love is not a cozy feeling. It is an act of the will. And the question remains, for you and for me, "What am I, *as a Christian*, to do?"

In the name of the Father, and of the Son, and of the Holy Ghost, Amen.

Part Five:

An Ethic Applied: Sin, Violence, Money, Sex, Politics, Environment

Thinking Theologically About Modern Life: Sin

Romans 7:7-25

Some years back I taught a Bible study on Matthew in two groups. The plan, which we accomplished, was to read the whole Gospel of Matthew with Tom Long's commentary in one hand for the tough questions. One group was well attended and met in the evenings on Wednesdays at seven. The other group met on Thursdays at noon and was designed to allow the parents of our preschoolers to come to Bible study for an hour before time for pickup. That is not remotely what happened. My daytime group turned out to be three women in their mid-eighties. At first, they were concerned that it was an inconvenience for me to teach a class for three people, but I assured them that I was going to do the same amount of preparation either way and so they assured me in turn that they would be in my study, like clockwork, every Thursday at noon until – and I promise you this is a direct quote – until one of them began dating a man who could drive after dark. At which point they intended to join my nighttime group.

One thing quickly became clear – in the privacy of my study, it was no holds barred. I still distinctly remember the time that one brought in the worship bulletin from the week before and, pointing to the prayer of confession said to me, "I can't pray this. I didn't *do* any of those things!"

We were discussing *sin* and this prompted another to respond, "Am I *really* a sinner? I know that's what the church teaches, but I keep all of the commandments, I try to be a good person, I come to church, I tithe… what *exactly* makes me a sinner?

That's a good question.

The church does indeed teach that we are all sinners, but are we all bad people? Indeed, in the Presbyterian Church, if you remember that old Calvinist acrostic TULIP that spells out the key doctrines, the very first is *total depravity*.

Not exactly a ringing endorsement for a grand vision of humanity.

While there are days where I would vouch that the drivers around me are in fact, completely and totally depraved, that's not what it means.

To be a sinner does not mean that you are a bad person. To acknowledge total depravity, in the Calvinist sense of meaning, does not mean we are as bad as we can possibly be.

To acknowledge that we are sinners is to recognize that something is broken that we can't fix for ourselves. To acknowledge *total depravity* is recognize that there's nothing in our lives that is exempt from the effects of sin.

Sin is a tough topic. To think of it means we have to look at what is wrong – in the world, in our lives, in our relationships. Nothing about talking about sin is easy. Indeed, in the preface to his wonderful book, <u>Not the Way It's Supposed to Be, a Breviary of Sin</u>, Cornelius Plantinga acknowledges that to look deeply into sin, one risks being unable to get back out.

But if we're going to think seriously, theologically, about such important matters as violence, sex, money, politics, and ecology, we need a foundation.

We need to understand sin.

Here is how I propose we proceed today: I am going to talk about sin in three ways: as a broken relationship with God, as defacement of the imago dei, and as vandalism of Shalom. We will not be able to cover the length and width of Christian thought on sin – this is merely a primer. And perhaps most importantly, we will not end with sin, we will end with redemption because that is the way in which God intends us to end.

So let's begin with sin as a broken relationship.

In the nineteenth century, there was an analogy for God that became rather popular with a school of thought called *deism* that suggested that God is a disinterested party where creation is concerned – God made creation and set it running and retired to a distance to watch us tick. Essentially, God was portrayed as a cosmic clockmaker who put it all together, started it running and stepped aside.

The problem with this analogy should be obvious to anyone who has read the opening chapters of Genesis. That's not the way the story went.

Now the story of how we came to be is not natural history. It's not intended to be. From the Genesis creation stories, we are intended to draw some broad theological conclusions. And one of the most evident is that God is deeply, intimately involved in what God is creating. Indeed, the best translations of the Hebrew *Bereshit bara Elohim et hashamayim ve'et ha'arets* which begins our Bible is more like this, "At the start of it all, God began creating… "

God's creative activity isn't limited to a one-time event wherein it was all started and finished and God left, but rather, God started creating and God keeps creating. God is not done with creation.

Creation is God's ongoing activity, and so it is God's ongoing relationship with everything.

And yet the story goes that we rebelled.

Classically, this is often called the fall and it forms the basis for much of the medieval theology of original sin with which the church struggled. It is an interesting side eddy, to my mind, so we are not going to talk about it today.

What is important for us to know is that in the beginning, God started creating the world in which we live and we are created with the intention of a good relationship with God who is intimately involved in the creation – at every stage, God proclaimed creation created and called it good, but when it came to humans, God breathed the breath of life into our clay. There's a big difference between proclamation and the intimate act of breathing life into the creature. That's the sort of relationship God wanted and God wants.

And then the story goes, we wanted more.

God created us for genuine community, but we wanted more.

That may just be sin in a nutshell. God created us to be human – in the image of God – but we wanted more, to be as God – to be creators for ourselves not reliant on God's goodness.

Perhaps it doesn't sound so bad, does it? All we really wanted was autonomy. All we really wanted was to be independent… to be our own people…. by ourselves… the rugged individual…

But that's not what God made us to be.

It brings us to the second point about sin that we need to understand. Sin is the defacement of the *imago dei*. In the same pages of scripture where we read about the creation we read as well that God made humanity in God's image.

Now, theologians disagree on this one – but I find most compelling the belief that when God made us in God's image it is that we are made to be in communion with God and with each other. Without going too deeply in to the finer points of Trinitarian theology, God has defined God's very own being in such a way that connectedness and community is who God is – we use the language of Father, Son and Holy Ghost in order to understand the persons of the trinity, and yet we affirm at the same time that God is one. God's very own understanding of self is of inextricable, inviolable community. And God made us in God's image.

When we make a declaration of independence from God and each other, we deface that image.

I mentioned theologians disagree on this one – the disagreement is primarily about whether or not what it means to be in God's image is to be made for a fellowship of love. The reason I find this definition so compelling is because of the words of Jesus – when asked what is the greatest commandment, what is the heart of the Law that God gave to define God's people, the answer was a resounding affirmation of the relationship between God and humankind and each other – Jesus' turned us back to the heart of the law – back to the heart of God's way for God's people, and it looked just like what God created in creation – love God, love each other… all of the time. That's what it means to be human. To be fully human, to live fully as God created us to live means to live in inviolable fellowship with one another and God. Anything less defaces God's image.

And that brings us to our third point about sin.

The broken relationship with God defaces God's image in us and it leads us to the vandalism of Shalom.

Shalom is more than merely a greeting, though many of us hear it that way. Shalom as a greeting is a well-wishing, a hope that the hearer will experience the peaceable well-being that comes only from God.

It may be a bit simplistic to think of it this way, but if the broken relationship with God and the defacement of God's image within our humanity represents sin as a state of being from which we cannot escape, then the vandalism of shalom represents sin as action – the actions that harm ourselves and others – and destroy the well-being that God wishes for the world. Sin as the vandalism of shalom is the consequence of placing ourselves above God and neighbor. War, lust, covetousness, murder, lies – these are the actions which condemn us.

Perhaps it is helpful to borrow an analogy from medicine. The first two – broken relationship and defacement of God's image, they are the disease. The last, vandalism of Shalom, is the symptom.

They're all deadly.

No matter whether symptom or disease, sin cuts us off from God.

But, you might think to yourself, I don't do any of those things. I'm free of lust, I don't support war, I've never murdered anyone, and I tell the truth.

We still all live in a world that is marred and disfigured by sin. When we participate in any way in broken creation, we participate in sin.

This isn't as good as it gets. God created us for better.

Sin is not the way it is supposed to be. Even if there isn't visible vandalism of Shalom, the fabric of what God has made isn't being made stronger.

When we participate in a way of life that is less than God wants, that is sin.

It may seem odd that in a sermon on sin I have managed to avoid mentioning the really juicy stuff – you know, fornication, adultery, usury, lying, cheating, stealing, the list could go on and on. Whatever they are, they are at their heart the result of the underlying problem of sin. It's really just a question of degrees.

Which is not to say that some sins aren't more hurtful than others. They are. But it is to say that whatever the sin is it's still sin.

I hope the end result of this treatment hasn't been to take something that is nasty, hurtful, demeaning, degrading and destroying and turn it into a garden-variety annoyance.

It would be so easy to think that it's just not a big deal.

Not if we have any idea of who God is.

God is holy. And God is the creator God who is still creating. Sin cuts us off from what is holy. Sin cuts us off from God. Sin cuts us off from the full humanity that God wills for us.

But here is the good news of the Gospel: God does not reject us. Whatever the nature of our sin, God does not reject us.

Maybe it's our sinful nature overruling the humanity for which God created us, but we seem so much to be obsessed with the sin of others. So much of what hurts, degrades and humiliates us is the sin that, to borrow a phrase from Paul, clings to us so closely.

I love the old chestnut that says, "Don't judge me because I sin differently than you do."

We may reject others because of the sin we perceive, but God does not reject them. We may reject ourselves because of our own sin, but God does not reject us.

Indeed, that is the heart of the Gospel, God does not reject us.

That is grace.

Whatever our faith teaches us about sin, whatever we have to say about the brokenness of our relationship with God and with each other, whatever word we have to say about the vandalism of Shalom and the defacement of the imago dei, it is a subordinate word because it always stands under the Word of God that supersedes our sin.

Sin is powerful. And sin is ugly. But there is more grace and mercy in God than there is sin in us.

There are many analogies that are used for grace: some liken it to winning the lottery without having bought a ticket. I love this threefold definition: grace is the unmerited, unearned, unconditional love of God.

Paul Tillich says it this way,

"Grace is the reunion of life with life, the reconciliation of the self with itself. Grace is the acceptance of that which is rejected. Grace transforms fate into meaningful destiny; it changes guilt into confidence and courage. There is something triumphant about the word 'grace': in spite of the abounding of sin, grace abounds much more."[48]

---

[48] Paul Tillich. *The Shaking of the Foundations*. (Scribners: NY, 1948) p 156

Sin matters. Grace exceeds sin.

If you have ever been terribly wronged, you know that the answer, "Oh it was nothing, don't worry about it," is a lie and it rings false.

God's answer to sin is not false. In Jesus Christ, God took all of the brokenness, defacement and vandalism of sin onto God's own self so that we would no longer have to bear it. That is grace.

We have an empty cross in our sanctuary to remind us of it. The cross is empty but it wasn't always. And that is the point. Whatever we have to say about sin, whether we are talking about sex, money, politics, ecology, violence – or whatever – we say it in light of that empty cross. Anything less cheapens it. Anything less is not grace.

In the name of the Father, and of the Son, and of the Holy Ghost, Amen.

Thinking Theologically About Modern Life: Violence
Romans 12:9-21; Luke 10:25-37

This past Monday I had lunch with a colleague and we began discussing the problem of violence.

I think we all can agree that violence is bad.

The disagreements start shortly thereafter as to what is just harmless fun, what constitutes dangerous violence and what must be avoided at all costs.

I'm being obtuse. My colleague quickly pointed out to me the pervasiveness of violence in our culture. If you think of it, we begin encountering violence at an early age. As soon as the anvil hits Wile E. Coyote's head we have our first encounters with violence. And interestingly, the crushed skull of Wile E. always reinflates and everything is fine.

You can take a riff on this and cover most of children's cartoons, at least the ones I remember. Tomcat, the original one, regularly falls victim to the machinations of Jerry and whatever the bulldog's name is. Bugs Bunny sticks his finger in the end of Elmer Fudd's shotgun and rather than blowing his hand off, it explodes in Fudd's face.

But surely there is a far cry from the harmless violence of Warner Bros. to the pornographic violence of the most problematic, adult only rated video games.

The last time I was in Charlotte I stayed with my sister and her family. My nephew wanted me to play Super Mario Brothers with him. It's about the only thing that carries over from my childhood to his, so we did. After it was time for him to go to bed, my sister and I stayed up to close to 2 a.m. trying to beat the various levels of the video game, shooting fireballs at the goombas, those little video creatures, stomping on their heads, and using whatever other tricks we could to decimate their population and I can assure you, we bear no moral scars for the goomba carnage that was left in our wake.

We know the difference, I think, between what is harmless and what is fatal. Only a moralistic pedant would equate harmless children's games with the soul-consuming problem of gun violence and the corporate killing of endless war.

We know the difference between harmless and fatal, but what about everything in between?

We know the difference, but where is the fine line between harmless teasing and deplorable bullying?

We know the difference between harmless and fatal, but when does a courageous act cease to be a protective act and turn instead to vindictiveness?

We may very well not be able to answer these questions today. I am by no means assured that Christian faith means we always know that what we are doing is the best path or even the most righteous path, but can rest in the assurance that in following Jesus we may at least seek the better way.

In order to have some framework around our thinking today, it may be helpful once again to break the problem down into component parts. These aren't exhaustive, but perhaps we can think of violence as a cognitive problem, then a verbal problem, and finally a physical problem.

Let's start with cognitive violence.

I am not a hundred percent certain that this sermon will pass philosophical, logical muster because I'm not one hundred percent certain that we can universalize this claim, but when I speak of cognitive violence, I am thinking of the ways in which we put categories in place to understand the world in which we live. A certain amount of categorization is understandable, perhaps even necessary just to get by. What I mean by this is, for example, that I'm here at Morningside, you're here at Morningside, and together we make a claim about what we believe. Say it's our commitment to hospitality and welcome. By being part of the same group, we can generalize a claim that we see the Biblical mandate to hospitality with some degree of commonality. There's nothing wrong with that. We share together a common value. It unites us.

We do this in all manner of matters.

What becomes problematic is when the categories become a way of reinforcing otherness.

There's nothing wrong with believing that fellow Morningsiders share a common value of hospitality. But if we in turn heard that – I'll just make this up – that the members of Podunk Episcopalian Church have taken to baptizing cats, and here at Morningside, we question the wisdom of baptizing cats.

But then if we in turn generalize that Episcopalians baptize cats we would head down a very wrong, very unhelpful path.

And if we decided that the Episcopalians were, in turn, unclean because of their liturgically suspect practice of baptizing cats, we've spun out of control.

And yes, I do get that there is absolutely everything in the world wrong with that analogy, but my point is this: whatever violence happens in the world, it begins with cognitive violence.

We make wrong assumptions. We divide the world into like and not like.

And then when physical violence happens it is the tragic living out of that cognitive violence.

It will take a trial to determine guilt in the Trayvon Martin case, but it wouldn't be too great a stretch to think that somewhere in this tragic altercation, there was cognitive violence that preceded the physical violence.

It's not accidental that when Jesus told this story of senseless violence on the Jericho road he used as his object lesson a man who would have been seen as decidedly *other*.

Good sense may on occasion necessitate a differentiation between self and other, but probably not as often as we think.

And it generally starts of innocently enough. My siblings and I can remember riding with my wonderful grandmother – this was back when electric door locks were a big deal in cars, and as we were riding down the road, clearly going 45 miles an hour or so, whenever my grandmother saw someone who seemed the least bit suspicious, she would reflexively press the button on the door of her Oldsmobile to be sure the doors were locked. Those locks were as loud as a shotgun blast. 45 miles per hour, and bam. It was an easy aural cue: like, and not like, self and other.

It's cognitive violence because if we are wrong, we are doing violence to the humanity of whomever we're creating our working generalizations about.

We don't know people for who they are, we know them for who we think they are. That reduces them, and ultimately, it reduces us. Remember that to be truly human is to be made for good relationship with God and with neighbor.

It's no wonder that when Jesus told the story of the merciful traveler, it was an outsider who helped.

Jesus called us to the ministry of the reconciliation of the world. Perhaps that reconciliation starts in our heads.

Monitor your thoughts. Check them for faithfulness to God's call to reconciliation. Remember Jesus' teaching to love the Lord our God and to love our neighbors. In so doing, we recover a little bit of our humanity.

Sometimes our thoughts spill out of our mouths.

When what spills out of our mouths is the overflowing of love, it's a wonderful thing to hear.

Most of the time, what spills out of our mouths is neither helpful nor harmful.

Some of the time, what spills out is the cognitive violence given voice.

Not too long ago I was watching television and I saw one of those NBC news specials that highlighted the problem of bullying.

They had test-cases where good kids were put in a room with bullying actors. It was amazing to see what happened.

Almost all of the kids struggled with what to do. Peer pressure overwhelmed some, others simply held back and a small minority were secure enough in themselves to speak out on behalf of the one who was being verbally violated.

Bullying, we hear, has reached epidemic proportions. It's verbal violence.

I have a hard time justifying the mindset of innocent school rites of passage. I also have a hard time throwing young people under the jail for bad judgment. So here is my meddling word for parents and it is the same meddling word that I have for bosses and it is the same meddling word I have for kids:

Be mindful of what goes in your head for fear it will come out of your mouth.

Words can hurt or words can heal. We have a twenty-four-hour entertainment cycle wherein words fill the air, sometimes masquerading as news, sometimes as entertainment. There is not an excuse for listening to words that hurt. It is poison in your brain. When we hear the diminishment of the humanity of any person for any reason, know it for the sin that it is.

Bullying has to have a context to become epidemic. I am sure that it is not remotely coincidental that the rise of false outrage as entertainment appears at the same time as a problem with bullying.

Mind your thoughts, because they may spill out of your mouth.

Mind your mouth because it may motivate action.

Remember Jesus' teaching to love the Lord our God with all our hearts, with all our minds and all our strength and to love our neighbors as ourselves.

Finally, we come to the problem of physical violence.

And in this instance, I have to confess my rank hypocrisy in that I remember two violent acts in my life with no small measure of pride.

The first is the time as an adolescent when I finally knocked the kid who had been shoving me in gym into the following week. Only the fear of having to stand in the lunchroom as an inmate of in-school suspension kept me from leaping on him to exact my revenge once it became clear that it had, in fact, worked.

The second was the one and only bar-brawl I have ever participated in, which occurred when I was in seminary, of all places, when a very drunken Princeton Graduate student kept trying to touch a woman in our group in inappropriate and unwelcome ways. Another classmate of mine and I stepped in between and he shoved and I shoved back.

It helps if you have to shove someone if they are intoxicated. They fall easily and you become a hero in your own mind.

I confess these because they seemed so incredibly justifiable. They still do.

And that's the problem with physical violence – so often it seems justifiable.

Very rarely are we violent for enjoyment. That would be sociopathic. No, the sin of violence must be more seductive.

We are, after all, civilized people. Therefore, violence must seem to arise out of necessity.

And yet the violence we do to others does violence to our humanity… Indeed, remember what God made us to be: for communion with God and with each other. And Jesus reminded us yet again, what it means to be in communion with neighbor.

Indeed, our calling to humanity may seem impossible. Paul makes it worse when he writes, "render to no one evil for evil… never avenge yourselves, leave room for God's wrath… live peaceably with all."

About the only part of that which seems easy is to feed our enemies because Paul tells us that in so doing we will heap burning coals on their heads. I can identify with that part. The rest seems impossible.

And yet. And yet.

We worship the prince of peace.

We read of God's vision for the peaceable kingdom, you know wolves and lambs lying down together, children and snakes playing together and no one gets hurt.

All of that peaceable kingdom stuff sounds like so much nonsense until we remember that it is God's vision for us.

This was originally going to be the war sermon. I have one from years ago from way back when the war in Iraq started.

But war is simply violence on a larger scale. The lessons hold. Thoughts lead to words lead to actions.

But I know as well that life tumbles in. War happens whether we want it to or not sometimes, and sometimes despite our greatest protestations.

I remember well a story I heard a while back of the return of a military brigade to the town that sponsored it during the middle ages. As the word arrived that the brigade was coming home, the townspeople lined the streets up the main road into the village, up the hill, to the cathedral. As the weary warriors entered the city, they marched resolutely past their silent fellow villagers. Finally, they reached the doors on the cathedral and entered. The townspeople filed in behind and together, collectively, the soldiers and their town confessed their sin and sought God's forgiveness. And only then, after acknowledging the sin of war, did the celebrations begin. That is the right posture of the Christian toward war. That is the right posture of the Christian toward violence.

You see violence is not the way it's supposed to be.

Mind your thoughts, they become words. Mind your words, they lead to action.

Let me close with a quotation a friend of mind reminded me of not too long ago, from Philo if Alexandria. He said, "Be kind. For everyone you meet is fighting a hard battle."

That battle, my friend said, is to hold on to our humanity.

Indeed it is. It is our humanity that God has called to reconcile the world.

In the name of the Father, and of the Son, and of the Holy Ghost, Amen.

Thinking Theologically About Modern Life: Money

Luke 12:41-48

Well, now. If you're interested in being eligible for the light beating, you should probably leave now, though I can't be certain you're not already in too deep for having heard the lesson. Eva and Carolyn still have a chance, I think, but if we raise them in the church like we've just pledged to help David and Emilee do, we're setting them on a collision course with what some might see as a hard reality.

Since Christian faith isn't just about life after death, it's about life *now*, the hard reality is that Christian faith actually has something to say about how we live our lives – including our money.

There's an old preacher's joke about the difference between preaching and meddling.

As the preacher is preaching the congregation is tracking along, affirming the message of the preacher with loud "amens" up until the point when he or she begins to get specific. The joke ends with one occupant of the "amen pew" leaning over to the other and remarking, "well, now he's done preaching and gone to meddling."

Up until now, we've only been talking about sin and violence. Now, though, we're about to get into the deep water, or at least so it feels to me. Now we're going to talk about money, sex and politics in the next few weeks and well, let's just say that it might start to sound like meddling.

My aunt used to work for a bank and she always said, "if you want to make people mad, start talking about their money."

So, how does a Christian relate to money?

You may have heard that money is the root of all evil. That's actually a misquote, if you've heard it that way. The quote is from the Bible, but it reads, "The love of money is the root of all kinds of evil."[49]

We can probably recount where all sorts of things have run terribly amok because of the love of money. Indeed, if we revisit the way we conceived of

---

[49] 1 Timothy 6:10

sin a few weeks back, as the state wherein we live with a broken relationship with God, we deface the image of God on us as good creations, and vandalize the good purposes for which God created us, for right relationship with God and neighbor, we can probably find some pretty good examples of those latter two based on actions motivated by the love of money.

What we do with our money either contributes to the *shalom* of the world or doesn't.

So there are three primary points I want to explore about money and Christian faith today. The first is that what we do with it matters. And the second is that we don't need to think about money and faith with fear. Finally, the claim of Christian faith on our financial lives needn't be motivated by guilt either.

What we do with our money can in fact be very moral or very immoral, but the state of being of having money or not having money is value neutral. What we do with what we have is what renders spiritual value.

When we make mistakes with money it tends to be because we've forgotten that it can have spiritual value.

Human beings have long had a pernicious tendency to divide the world into things that are material and things that are spiritual.

This is a false dichotomy.

What do I mean by this? I mean that we tend to divide our lives into material and spiritual compartments – things like prayer, worship, in some cases study go into a category that we term spiritual. We have no problem identifying the value of these spiritual things. And then we lump other things into a material category that we deal with but don't think of spiritually. Money tends to be placed into this second category.

This false dichotomy goes back to the Hellenization of the ancient near east. With the Greeks came the idea that there were material realms and spiritual realms and they are somehow separate from one another. That which was deemed spiritual was of finer stuff and deserved our attention and that which was deemed material was bad, grubby and lesser and should merely be tolerated. Thought and prayer would be something spiritual and money and sex would be decidedly material.

The problem with this viewpoint for a Christian is that it is decidedly unchristian. If we look seriously to the Hebrew roots of our faith, we will see that God makes no such distinction between "good" creation and "bad" creation. When God makes the world, it's all good. Indeed, God got down into the midst of the material in creating human kind – remember, we weren't simply commanded into existence, we were created into existence by the intimate act of God breathing life into us. So there isn't a bit of creation that doesn't have God's fingerprints all over it.

There isn't an aspect of our lives where God doesn't want intimate relationship with us.

God wants us to relate to every aspect of our lives from a spiritual standpoint because God didn't divide the world into spiritual and material – so what we do with our money matters.

God made this wonderful good creation and set us into the midst of it as God's caretakers.

The terms "steward" and "stewardship" have become church-speak. In the last couple of centuries, they have come to be associated with the raising of money for church operations. We've lost something in limiting the concept of stewardship thusly. So, let me say about word about the steward.

The steward, in Biblical usage, refers to the person who is tasked with and charged with responsibly managing the assets of a household, which could be very large. The steward is an elevated figure in the household – indeed, the master has entrusted the most important of responsibilities to the steward. It is good thing to be the steward.

In our own households, we're stewards of what we have. We may be good or bad stewards, but we are entrusted with what God has given us. In the household of the church, our session are the stewards of what God has given this congregation by way of our annual commitment campaign. (I love that we call it, "commitment," because it says it's not just about raising and spending money, but it's about how we commit to one another to be present with each other and to help those of us with children to raise them in the faith, and those of us who are aged to have companionship and for all of us to gather together in worship and be inspired and lifted up. That's something I can commit to!)

God has given us abundance and from that abundance we have taken what we need. That is as God intends it to be. Inasmuch as the way we steward our resources contributes to the shalom of the world, it is exactly as God intended it to be.

But passages such as we read today can be a touch frightening though, can't they?

When we are fearful that our stewardship might leave us cruising for a bruising, no wonder it is comforting to divide the world into spiritual and material!

So, if our decisions about money and faith are motivated by fear, we need to back up.

I picked this passage to go with this sermon because I suspect that most, if not all of us, have at some point or another in our lives harbored at least a slight secret fear that these parables might, in fact, be evidence that God is secretly just a hair-trigger away from whomping us.

That is not the point of this parable or any others like it. Taken within its larger context, this parable points us to the reminder that God is the gracious source of all that we have. Indeed, the hymn we will sing later is Matthew's version of the same words. "Consider the lilies, consider the ravens, does not God provide for them?"

When Luke includes such a story it is because he wants to intensify the claim of the Gospel on us – take this seriously, he seems to be saying. Indeed, Jesus is asked by his followers, "do you mean this about us?"

Yes. He does. He does mean it for us.

But he doesn't mean it to scare us. He means it to help us get the seriousness of it, to remember that there is more to this world than the acquisition and disposition of stuff.

And also, whatever the Bible has to say about God's hope and expectations of how we should relate to the world with our money, it does so while unabashedly declaring that we are the subjects of tremendous grace.

Everything we have, indeed, everything we are – is a gift from God.

That should leave us with no question of whether or not God loves us.

So, we don't need to relate to money out of fear that God is going to whomp us. That's not the point of the parable and it's not the point of the Gospel.

So what we do with our money shouldn't be motivated by fear, it should be motivated by what we can do that is *good*. And that is the heart of living like God has blessed us.

Which brings me to that last part, not acting out of guilt.

Again, I have to confess my rank hypocrisy. I once made my pledge to my local NPR affiliate because I realized that I had memorized the phone in number for the pledge-line. I had been listening for free for so long that I was even suffering through the pledge drive, so much was my addiction. I had the epiphany that I was a free-loader.

But this isn't NPR and I'm not Ira Glass. We're about the business of church here and this is a place of grace. While it is my deep hope that the members of this church live our lives out of gratitude and in so doing that the response to that gratitude is generosity to the church and our communities, what we do needn't – indeed, shouldn't – be motivated by guilt.

Let me tell you a story. I remember well a couple in Indianapolis that I knew many years back. Bill and Chris were their names and they were just delightful. By the time I met them Chris was in her late eighties and Bill was in his early nineties. She had a gold Mercedes convertible that Bill bought her for "their golden years" and she would ride around with their dog, Lance, in the backseat with the top down Bach blaring over the speakers. I have it on good authority that Lance Jr. once had his own seat on the Concorde. (I only met Lance IV but he was very well behaved.)

Bill had founded a law firm that cornered the market on one particular discipline of the law and excelled in it. He made the comment to me once, "I used to feel guilty about the fact that I've been financially successful, but then I realized that I could do a lot of good with the money I've made. I don't really have any gifts for teaching Sunday School, nor the desire, or to volunteer to sort clothing for the clothes closet, but I am very good at making money. And I sort of think that's my contribution to the church!"

I love to tell that story about Bill and Chris, partly because they were just so much fun to be around, but also because it highlights the truth that when we live our lives with gratitude rather than guilt, God can do wonderful things.

So let's be clear: by definition, the recipients of grace are free-loaders. By definition! That's the way God wants it! God didn't set up a world where we have to earn God's love, God continually gives freely from the overflowing of God's love.

We'll never out-give God. Try it if you like, but God will always be more generous!

That's the great good news of the Gospel! That's what we're here to proclaim over and over again, in sermon and song, to young and old: that God made the world out of the overflowing of God's love, and that God redeemed us because God wants a good relationship with us and wants us to have a good relationship with each other.

It's not a trap! It's not bait and switch! It literally is what it is and is not something else.

So, that's the word I have from the Lord about money.

> 1. There's not a single part of our lives God isn't interested in. Including our money – and what we do with it gives it meaning.

> 2. God doesn't want us motivated by fear.

> 3. God doesn't want us motivated by guilt.

If there is a carry away from this sermon for you to live your life by this week – about money or anything else, it's this: it's all a gift from God.

So here's your homework: live with joy. And live with generosity.

In the name of the Father and of the Son, and of the Holy Ghost, Amen.

Thinking Theologically About Modern Life: Sex
1 Corinthians 13

So, let's start with a story.

A preacher goes to a new call at a new church in a one stop-light sort of town. (This is not an autobiographical story in any way. I've never lived in a small town.) When he arrives to his new call, the only church in town, his sole means of transportation is his bicycle. So, you can imagine he was absolutely devastated when his bike went missing within the first few weeks of his arrival. He was inconvenienced by this loss of his transportation, but more than that, he was devastated by the nature and character of Christian community of his new town – his is the only church, so he concludes the thief must be a member of his new congregation.

He calls an extraordinary meeting of the elders of the church and tells them of the theft and how it has shattered his view of his fellow townspeople. One of the elders intrepidly offers a plan.

"Pastor," he says, "You are right. Ours is a small community and this is the only church. So certainly the thief must be here on Sundays. If you confront the congregation with the theft, the thief will know something is up and hide the bike. So I propose this solution: preach a sermon on the Ten Commandments. When you get to 'thou shalt not steal,' bear down really hard on that one. Elaborate on the punishments of hell that await such ne'er do wells, and as you do, look around at the congregation. Surely the one who is guilty will be squirming with the awareness of what the consequences of his actions may be. That way, you will know who the thief is and we can recover your bike."

The preacher and the elders murmur amongst themselves and conclude that this is a brilliant plan.

Sunday morning arrives and the preacher is in fine form. He is preaching up a storm on the Ten Commandments and the perils of hell when suddenly, he ends the sermon, pronounces the benediction and abruptly leaves the sanctuary.

A few minutes later the elders follow him to the manse, absolutely eaten up by curiosity. Finally, one of the elders voiced their question, "Preacher, it was going so well – I was even becoming a little afraid of hell myself and I didn't steal the bike – why did you stop?"

"Well," the preacher replied while shoving clothes into a suitcase, "I was preaching my way toward, 'thou shalt not steal,' but as soon as I got to 'thou shalt not commit adultery,' I remembered where I left my bike."

The moral of this story is this: whatever we have to say about sin, in any form, we do well to begin by looking at ourselves first.

I begin with this caution because for reasons that we will discuss in a moment, sex and the discussion of morality and sin surrounding it, seems to draw a disproportionate level of interest and indeed judgment in the modern church.

Recently I read Ann Patchett's wonderful novel, <u>The Patron Saint of Liars</u>. It is a beautiful novel and it was set in a home for unwed mothers in Kentucky in the last century. What often struck me was the sense of shame and disgrace that was visited on the young women in the story.

Indeed, shame and disgrace seems to be a recurrent theme in the church's treatment of sex and sexuality. To read it and in fact to hear about it from persons of a certain age is to remember a period in which the norms were very closely and tightly defined and any variance from the norm – an unwed pregnancy, or a physical and emotional attraction to a person of the same gender – might indeed bring disgrace upon one and one's family.

And indeed, if **dis**grace is what we remember, then we know that it arises out of the shortage of grace, not from God, but from ourselves for each other.

If the church is to be a place of honesty about the myriad issues of sex and sexuality, we must also be a place of grace. Even as I stand here, I am monumentally aware that we range in personal history from those who have no experience sexually, to those who waited for marriage, to those for whom marriage is not an option but a life of covenant commitment is, to those who have a great deal of experience but have perhaps received little commitment. For all of us, Jesus Christ offers grace upon grace, with no qualification for receiving it. Indeed, to read the stories of the Bible is to see a God who offers grace – unconditional love – to the whole of creation.

So any theological conversation about sex will be grounded in grace.

With that said, the Bible and faith have a lot to say about sex. What I'd like for us to do for the next few minutes is first to reflect on the context of scripture for a while, and then to consider what claims our faith may place upon our lives. Finally, I want us to end by remembering that the physical expression of love is a gift from God.

So, let's place a little context around scripture. There is a fair amount about sex in the early parts of the Bible. And we don't worship a capricious God, so there is a reason for many of the prohibitions surrounding sex in the Bible. I'm going to try to cover a lot of ground here, so this is going to involve some gross simplifications. Basically, the issues that lead to much of what we encounter in the first five books of the Bible are idolatry, property rights, and the maintenance of creation.

First idolatry – this one may seem a surprise, but remember this: Yahweh, the God of Sarah, Rebekah, Leah and Rachel, as well as their husbands, Abraham, Isaac and Jacob, is a jealous God who tolerates no rivals for worship. This is pretty plainly stated. And yet the Hebrews and proto-Hebrews lived in places where the indigenous pagan religions were religions centered on fertility. What this means is that the people all around God's people were concerned with ensuring the fertility of the earth by participating in rituals around fertility. I'm trying to be delicate here, but essentially what it boils down to is that the people God was trying to form into God's people were surrounded by alternate opportunities, shall we say, for worship in the form of cultic expression of sexuality. Which is to say that a male would go to the "temple" and there meet a "priestess" who would help him to participate in the fertility cycle of the earth, thus pleasing the gods and goddesses who assured the continual cycle of birth, death and rebirth that surrounded the agriculture of the day.

The Hebrews were the beginning of the radical notion of monotheism, and the God of the Hebrews, our God, took no delight in cultic prostitution and forbade it for his people. So, much of the expression of sexuality that is being fenced out in the early books of the Bible is sexual expression tied to idolatry – the worship of other gods, in this case, through sexual practice.

Second, property rights – this one is pretty offensive by our standards today. Women were the property of their household, as were slaves and children. In some ways this served as a protection for their rights because God had expectations for the heads of households that are, in fact, laid out in the law. But the prohibition against adultery that we encounter in the Decalogue as well as elsewhere has to do with creating communities of trust and well-being where households function harmoniously within and peacefully without. And so in good communities with good relations, one did not steal the property of another household and violate it. That would destroy the shalom of the community. Our modern understanding of adultery as the violation of the covenant commitment that adults make to one another has very little to do with the ancient understanding of the preservation of the household for the preservation of the male line.

Now quickly that last problem of keeping creation going – this one has less to do with the bearing of children than it does with same-gender relations. In the early portions of Scripture, there is a thread of thought that is known as creation theology that is built around a conviction that creation is incredibly delicate and ordered and that only rigid maintenance of certain boundaries can prevent the devolution of creation back into the chaos from which God called it into order. Think of the days of creation of Genesis: on the first three days, God created places, and on the second three days, God created things to occupy those places. So there is a place for everything and everything is in its place. Through the maintenance of this order, the chaos, or formless void, is kept at bay. This is the source of a lot of the ritual ordering and abomination talk of such books as Leviticus and Numbers.

So that is a crash course in the issues that underpin the prohibitions surrounding sex in the Old Testament: avoidance of idolatry, preservation of property lines, and the maintenance of the created order.

Those are not the issues that the church is facing today. If these are your issues, I've got some books for you, but this isn't what we're facing today.

The issues that are important to us today are these, I think: in a world that sometimes seems hypersexualized and on occasion, cheap, how do I live my life with integrity and commitment, how do I teach my children if I have them, to grow up to be persons of integrity and commitment, and in the meantime, keep them from doing something really stupid that will alter the course of their lives dramatically.

Let's take these two in reverse order, starting with the kids.

Parents have an innate covenant commitment to seek the best for their children by virtue of choosing to have them. The rest of us have an acquired covenant commitment that we signed on to when we said "yes" to the baptismal vows when the babies are baptized. That covenant commitment is to help children to know who Jesus Christ is and what the Christian life is about and to be deeply and personally concerned for their wellbeing.

And perhaps one of the most important things we can realize is that children are not adults. So the content of what we see, say and hear is received differently by young people than it is by old people, which all of us over say, 20, should consider ourselves.

We all encounter more distorted images and expectations of sexuality than we probably should, but adults do so with a somewhat formed sense of ethic and identity.

Children and adolescents, on the other hand, are still in the process of forming ethics and identity. It is vitally important that the church be clear in its expression that sex and sexuality are not bad or sinful and yet sometimes something God meant for good can be made hurtful.

Here's where I meddle: if you are a parent, set the tone. Turn off "The Bachelor/ette" or whatever its current permutation is if it's on in your home. Explain that there is a difference between entertainment and commitment. Read a book about discussing sex with children if need be and answer questions with grace and kindness. If you need help formulating a Christian way to talk to your children about sex and sexuality, come to me and we will get together the parents who need information and get the experts in. We have made solemn vows to help you through this awkward age. We promised this and we will do it.

Now, back to the adults. I have set aside my own blushes and given you as candid a description as I can of what underpins much of what the Bible teaches about sex and sexuality. Let me close that portion of the sermon by saying much of the issues that the writers of the Old Testament were concerned about remained enough of a problem that Paul sought to establish some ground rules for the newly forming Christian churches that he ministered to through his correspondence. So, yes, Paul does deal with cultic ritual practice in his letters. And inasmuch as we don't worry with these things, some of what he has to say can sound antiquated. His point is good, "look, that's how the pagans do it, and you don't want to be confused with a pagan so act like this."

That's where some of the passages about women covering their heads comes from – I could go on, but I won't. It does seem though, that since our issues today are not ones of idolatry, property rights or single-handedly keeping chaos at bay from the world, that perhaps the source of a uniquely Christian sexual ethic for modern life can come not from teachings about how to avoid being confused with the pagans, but from what the Bible teaches about love.

Every aspect of what it means to be a child of God is grounded in love. Indeed, the imago dei – the image of God in which we are made – is the image of God as love. That is why the heart of the law and the Prophets, as Jesus said, is the commandment to love the Lord our God with all our heart, soul, mind and strength, and to love our neighbors as ourselves. That is what it means to be human.

And that is the basis for a *human* sexuality – that we seek to love God and love our neighbor. What that means is wanting the best for our neighbor. Where sex is concerned, that means an ethic that is grounded in love – not a shallow, facile understanding of love, but love like what Paul wrote about.

Paul wrote that wonderful hymn to love for a congregation that wasn't being very lovely. And that's important. Sometimes sex is the fullest expression of human love. And sometimes it is very unlovely. When it is the latter, we know our calling – to live love in ways that give witness to what we believe about Jesus Christ.

That's important. Because I worry sometimes that we can confuse grace – the free expression of God's unconditional love for us – with an "anything goes" mentality. And yet, God means our lives to be for the reconciliation of the world – that God is using us to show the ways in which God loves us.

You know what love is? Well, Paul didn't much seem to – he just described what love looked like: it's patient, kind, not envious or arrogant, or boastful or rude. It believes all things, hopes all things, endures all things.

When I said that I would preach this series, many folks commented to me that we'd have a full house today. One of my colleagues suggested that I should switch the sex and money sermons and not tell anyone. (I think you'd have noticed.) As I heard all of the jokes – and a few tips – that have been offered, I was musing with an old friend of mine – she's about eighty-four – about the interest that the sex sermon had garnered. And as I was talking about it, I said, "You know, everyone thinks that the sex sermon will be interesting. My goal now is to make it boring."

To which she dryly replied, "I assure you, it isn't."

That's rather the point. And that's how God intended it to be!

The full expression of love is a gift – and so God intended it to be.

In the name of the Father and of the Son, and of the Holy Ghost, Amen.

Thinking Theologically About Modern Life: Politics
Jeremiah 29:1-7

Well, a number of you have asked me if I will be telling you for whom to vote today.

The answer to that is a resounding no. In fact, if I do my job right, you might leave with some glimmer of a suspicion about my politics, but no more, and that only because none of us is completely without bias.

No, in a democratic republic that espouses separation of church and state, preaching a sermon on politics is probably almost as bad an idea as preaching a sermon on sex.

I spent far too much time selecting the tie I wore to church this morning – and I'm not often perplexed by sartorial conundrums. (I settled on a purple one.)

Indeed, some of you may have heard Tony Campolo's famous analogy about politics and faith, that it's something akin to mixing manure and ice cream. It doesn't much affect the manure, and it does little to improve the ice cream.

And of course, there was always H.L. Mencken's assessment: "No one in this world has ever lost money by underestimating the intelligence of the great masses of the plain people. Nor has anyone ever lost public office thereby."

Mencken was not such a great fan of human nature.

But I do think that the feelings of these thinkers are not so far from the mainstream. For many Christians today there is a sense that the political system is somehow full of deceit and back-dealing. For many Christians today, there is a tension between living a Christian life and voting. Indeed, for those who feel most passionately about the candidates who are standing for office this election season, come November 7th, some percentage of the populace will find themselves feeling something like exiles under a government democratically elected but not of their choosing.

Indeed, I am just about certain that no matter which way the election concludes members of *this* congregation will be excited or disappointed. We are not a homogenous congregation any more than we are a homogenous nation.

So what I'd like for us to think about today is how to be a Christian in a country going through a general election. To that end, I'd like to begin by identifying two ways in which we relate to government. Then I'd like for us to spend a few minutes thinking of some things Christians ought *not* to do before finally concluding with a few things that Christians ought to do.

To my mind, there are really two primary ways in which the Christian relates to government. The first is to seek to influence government, and the second is to eschew all things government. I'm not sure that either represents the right way to be all the time.

In the first model, Christians seek to influence government. This is the scenario in which religious beliefs are used to shape legislation. You have perhaps heard of the Women's Christian Temperance Union which lead to Prohibition. You have perhaps heard of the influence that the religious groups exerted on California's Proposition 8 some time ago. And of course, there was a time in our country's history when religion was used as the basis for anti-miscegenation statutes that forbade persons of different races from marrying one another.

Two of those look like really bad ideas in retrospect, and the jury is out on the other. But when religious viewpoints have been legislated on to other people to ill-effect, it should leave little wonder that the church struggles sometimes to find fertile soil to plant the Gospel.

When one is in the majority, it is easy to forget that one may not always be the majority and sometimes the majority is not right.

There was a time when the United States was governed by many Episcopalians and Presbyterians. At this moment, there is not a mainline Protestant on either Presidential ticket. There is not a protestant Christian on the US Supreme Court.

How it was is not how it ever shall be.

And I do realize that this is running dangerously close to being a civics lesson and not a sermon, so let me come straight to the point: Jesus' strongest condemnation in the Gospels seems often to be reserved for those who present themselves as authoritative in matters of faith practice for people other than themselves – namely, the Pharisees.

Now I know that the Pharisees were well meaning. Indeed, I know that I have defended them on occasion and will again. However, Jesus often identifies their well, *Pharisaical* behavior as highly problematic.

We do well to take that under advisement.

However, the stance of eschewing all things government also has its flaws. In the minor prophets, about which Drew is teaching an excellent series, we will readily find much of God's disfavor displayed for the belief that what we do doesn't matter to God, that nations can with impunity ignore the needs of people in their midst to the benefit of others. In order to construct a faith system wherein persons of faith are not responsible for the conduct of our common life together requires us to slash at our own holy text because the Bible is full of the expectation that we will seek to live in good and harmonious communities – indeed, the whole law seems to be founded upon the conviction that this is a good thing.

We have heard for the past five weeks straight some form of the Shema, an old Creed of Judaism, that forms the heart of the great Commandment: we are to love the Lord our God with all our heart, with all of our strength, with all of our soul and with all of our minds, and the second is like unto it, that we are to love our neighbors as ourselves.

John Calvin noted that the Decalogue could be divided into the first table of the Law and the Second table of the Law, with the first table, or commandments, being oriented toward how we relate to God and the second being oriented to how we relate to each other.

The very foundation of our faith assumes our commitment and expectation to work for good community.

Which is enough to leave a Christian in a political season in at least something of a quandary, no?

I must confess, with a certain amount of humility, that there is sufficient diversity in the Biblical witness as to how persons of faith relate to government that I am not sure that I can give a definitive answer to my own question. But I do think we can establish some helpful parameters, which brings us to what not to do.

This one is pretty easy to come up with. Remember what Mr. Rogers taught us about living in community: be kind to one another and respect one another.

There are any number of vilifying, disrespectful remarks that I have heard directed at persons running for political office. Socialist and Vulture Capitalist just jump right to mind as two of the sillier ones. Silly, but no less disrespectful and hurtful.

God is not pleased when we mock, malign, or in any way rundown any person for any reason at any time.

No part of that type of behavior is pleasing to God.

Which is not to say that persons of faith must live uncritically. We are certainly expected to use our brains and to be thoughtful. But God does assume we'll act like Christians while we're doing it.

The second is that as we are thinking critically about politics, we must remember not to be uncritical of ourselves. I seem to recall Jesus' words to some Pharisees about being able to see the splinter in someone else's eye while being oblivious to the plank in their own eyes. The teachings still apply.

Finally, when thinking critically about others and ourselves, we remember that judgment ultimately belongs to God, who does not tolerate rivals for the claim. Persons of faith will vote in many ways in this election, and perceived wrongness of political thought does not mean less faith or less conviction. God is always, ultimately in charge of the world, which, should my candidate lose, I'll take as a comfort.

There is plenty more of "what not to do." I read a good, if simplistic article a few weeks back in an online magazine named *Relevant* entitled, "Seven Things Christians Need to Remember about Politics." I commend it to your attention.

At the same time, though, we remember that God does not ever want us to be so concerned about getting it wrong that we do nothing. Which brings us to what *to* do.

I love that passage of Jeremiah that we read today. I particularly love the admonition to seek the welfare of the city where we are. In the Hebrew, it reads *Shalom*. We are to seek the *shalom* of the city where God has called us to be.

The city just means the community and it can be as large or as small as the political entity needs to be to include the whole community.

And God's word to that community that Jeremiah addressed was to seek the shalom of their community.

And what is so striking to me is that it is the community in which the Israelites are exiled.

So they weren't the dominant voice. Indeed, they weren't even a respected voice per se. And yet, God counsels them to seek the well-being of their community.

And that Word carries to us still.

Regardless of what a Christian believes about the role of government or the present or future incumbent of high office, the calling remains to seek the good, to seek what is better and to work diligently for that shalom for which God created us.

At the end of the day, no matter how passionately we feel about a candidate or party or popular movement, no matter how deeply disappointed we are when we lose or how jubilant we are when we win, we are still a community. We are a community of faith living in a community in need of reconciliation. And we're called to be the agents of reconciliation, as Paul reminded us in 2 Corinthians.

That's a big call. We'll need some fortification for it. We'll need to eat hearty and get up our strength.

Isn't it wonderful that there is a table set for us to do just that?

In the name of the Father, and of the Son, and of the Holy Ghost, Amen.

Thinking Theologically About Modern Life: The Earth
Genesis 1:24-31

Well, here we are at the end of the series. This was going to be called, "The ETC. Sermon," but as I thought of it, I'm not sure that many of us go around with a burning concern for the use of the term et cetera. Some may get worked up over its correct pronunciation, but we tend to spend our intellectual energy and our Christian vocation on tangible concerns. And as I thought of the things that call for a Christian response from us, I came around to the matter of environmental stewardship.

This was something of an improbable topic for me as I've never preached an *Earth* sermon. As environmentalists go, I'm pretty lax. Sure, I'm good about recycling and I have compact fluorescent light bulbs, but by and large, I couldn't pass a staunch environmentalist's litmus test.

A few years back I took an environmental assessment. At the time I lived in a small condo, drove a four-cylinder car and lived less than a mile and a half from work. I flunked it miserably, though. My carbon footprint was considered excessive. Now my house is bigger than I need, my car is probably just a little too powerful, and I drive three miles to work. I'm sure the standards haven't relaxed in the intervening years! That mix seems to me to be just tailor made for a first-class guilt trip. Which of course, would just add to my carbon footprint.

Add to that reality the additional complicating factor that matters of environmental stewardship have become something of a political football, and the result is possible paralysis when it comes to what we believe about the earth and how we live in it.

So today we will not wade into the policy debates. The Bible makes no recommendations where modern environmental issues are concerned. The ancient Hebrews had no knowledge of cap and trade policies and Jesus didn't drive a car.

To make a universal claim about environmental stewardship with any degree of specificity using the Bible as backup would require that claim to be so vague as to be nonsensical.

And yet, the opening chapters of Genesis make it very clear that God loves what God has made. God calls it good. And there is no mistaking the fact that God has placed humans into creation as stewards.

You remember what a steward is – it's someone who manages something that doesn't belong to them.

God doesn't give the world over to humankind to *have*, but rather, to *manage*.

And interestingly, God has some opinions about the management of what God has made.

I remember when I was a kid my grandfather had a garden. He would spend hours painstakingly maintaining it. My grandfather was a bit of a neat-freak, which I respect, and his rows of okra, green beans and corn were a sight to behold.

Later when I was older I was talking to my grandfather about his garden again. And he said the most amazing thing. Amidst saying he did this and that to prepare the soil, he added, "And I let the land rest every seventh year."

I was puzzled, and I said, "You let the land rest?"

"The Bible says to," he replied.

I went and looked it up.

The Bible does indeed say that the land is to rest ever seventh year.

This points to a God who does indeed care deeply about creation, and not just about the human creation that God has made, but about the whole of it, every speck of dust and blade of grass.

Some weeks back, when we were talking about money, a topic incidentally, that we're not through with yet, we considered a false dichotomy that persists in the world and is extraordinarily detrimental to the life of faith.

The false dichotomy was of course, between the material and the spiritual. In talking about money, I observed that there is a somewhat pernicious tendency to divide the world into spiritual things, like worship and prayer, and material things, such as money and politics. This dichotomy is false because God made the whole thing and God loves the whole thing and there isn't an aspect of our lives where God doesn't want deep and personal connection to us.

And that's true. That's who God is. God, in triune nature, exists in deep and indivisible unity as Father, Son and Holy Ghost. And to be made in God's image means to be made for deep unity and integration – in life and in community.

But there is another false dichotomy that is like unto the first, and it is this: it is to treat this world as being of inferior, grubby stuff, because it is temporal and something better is to come.

Now what I mean by this is not to say that there is not a difference between life now and the life to come. Not by a long shot. But that life to come is remarkably vague in scripture, and I think for good reason – we are to be concerned with life now and trust God for life later.

Which is to say we aren't done with this world until we're done with it.

We live here.

We're the stewards.

We are God's agents in the world. It's a little bit of a cliché to say we hold it in trust for the next generation, but clichés exist because they point to a truth. God *has* entrusted us with the care of what God has made and it is so that we will care for it *wisely*.

So, theologically, we know what not to do: we don't treat this world like it doesn't matter, because it does. It's not disposable.

But what are we to do? How do we live a uniquely Christian ethic with regard to the world in which we live? And moreover, how do we live that Christian ethic when it is abundantly clear that some of the solutions to the challenges of modern life lie seemingly not in the hands of individuals, but in the hands of corporations and government?

We know full well that the living out of our theological thought may take many different forms, but I think we can use two words to frame our thoughts. Those words are *gratitude* and *rectitude*.

If we are living lives of gratitude it will shape our actions.

Now I find this to be a true statement on a variety of topics. If we are living lives of gratitude for what God has done for us, we tend to be generous in our spirits. I never tire of thinking that every nickel this church spends in ministry and mission is spent because someone was motivated by gratitude to give it to service of God.

But where environmental stewardship is concerned, it goes deeper. When you are grateful for something, you treat it right. You make note of its condition and your obligation to care for it. Not to do so implies the opposite.

I have a clock in my living room. It came from my grandparents' home and my mother tells me that it came before that from my great-grandparents' home. After that the trail goes cold. But it's really old.

When this clock came into my possession it had sat on the mantle of my grandparents' home for many years in disuse for my entire life. No one thought it worked. But when I got it home, for just a few minutes, I heard rapid ticking. Not rhythmic, but machine-gun fire type ticking. I didn't think anything of it. And then I moved it to another shelf in my living room, and I heard the noise again. And I began to wonder, "Does this thing yet have life in it?"

I opened the back of it and found the winding key. I wound it up. Then I got non-stop rapid ticking, of the pneumatic drill variety, as in drilling in your brain, and I knew it would go on unless I did something about it. So I got a flashlight and looked into the casing – back in the recesses of the case I found the pendulum weight. I attached it. The clock slowed to a rhythmic *tick-tock, tick-tock*.

Eventually, after many months, it became erratic again and I took it to a clock-maker. He said, "It needs cleaning and care, but it will run just fine. What is its history?"

"Well, it was on the mantle in my grandparents' home for many years, and before that at my great-grandparents' home. I don't remember ever hearing it chime, but when we cleaned out the house, I asked for it. My parents took the grandfather clock and I got this little one."

"Well," he replied, "You got the more valuable piece by a wide margin."

I took the clock because it made me think of my grandparents. I cared for it because I loved them. And astonishingly, in caring for it, I realized it was worth a very great deal.

I share this little story because when we neglect something, it appears we don't think it's worth very much. In time, with enough neglect, it may come to appear not to *be* worth very much. But what it is – made by God, for good purposes – remains.

That's true of clocks. It's true of people. And it's true of the world God has entrusted to our care as well.

And I don't know, perhaps its Pollyanna thinking, but I can't help but believe if our posture of engaging the world in which we live is one of deep gratitude to God who has made it, if we won't find ourselves more cognizant of the ways in which our actions either give honor to what God has made, or give dishonor to what God has made. But as far as the Biblical witness goes, there can be no mistaking that what God has made, God loves.

Which brings me to rectitude. *Rectitude* is a word that seems to have fallen into disuse in recent years, and that's something of a shame, to my mind. It just means to be concerned with correctness and right behavior morally.

If we are grateful, we will live as though we recognize the value of what has been given into our care. And if we live grateful lives, we will live with a certain amount of rectitude.

Which seems to me to be natural the conclusion of our series.

It has no doubt come to your attention that some version of the great commandment has been the "other lesson" all six weeks. It appears three times in the New Testament and also in Deuteronomy. In Deuteronomy, it is the heart of the law, in the Gospels, it is Jesus' answer to the question, "what is the most important thing we can do?"

You know the words, "Love the Lord your God with all your heart, soul, mind and strength." And then Jesus adds, "And love your neighbor as yourself."

You see, for generations, the church has struggled to divine what God's will is for modern life. It goes back, way back, to our formatives years. Throughout our history, Christians have sought to take this holy text, which tells us of our God and the incarnation, and apply it to our lives.

In time, the early bishops began to discern a "rule of faith" for way of life for the believer. What it meant was that those who seek to understand how God would have us live in the world start with faith, with the teachings of the church and the scriptures.

In time, St. Augustine came to add what is called the "rule of love." In the preface to his monastic *Rule*, he wrote, "Before all else, beloved, love God and then your neighbor, for these are the chief commandments given to us."

Meaning, as we seek to understand our way in the world, we will be guided by love because it is for love that God has made us. A life of rectitude will necessarily be governed by faith, but more, it will be governed by love.

When it comes to understanding sin and violence, relating to money and sex, and making our way with politics and care for the environment, the way of gratitude in turn becomes the way of rectitude.

Friends, for the short span of six weeks we have delved into a way of thinking about our place as creatures that God has placed in the midst of a good creation where we will encounter such things that require us to use our minds. But the simple truth remains that, as much as our minds matter to God, so much more do our hearts. And living into this rule of faith and love will very well take our whole lives. But then, what else were we going to do?

In the name of the Father, and of the Son, and of the Holy Ghost, Amen.

www.ingramcontent.com/pod-product-compliance
Lightning Source LLC
Chambersburg PA
CBHW071330120626
46546CB00002B/511